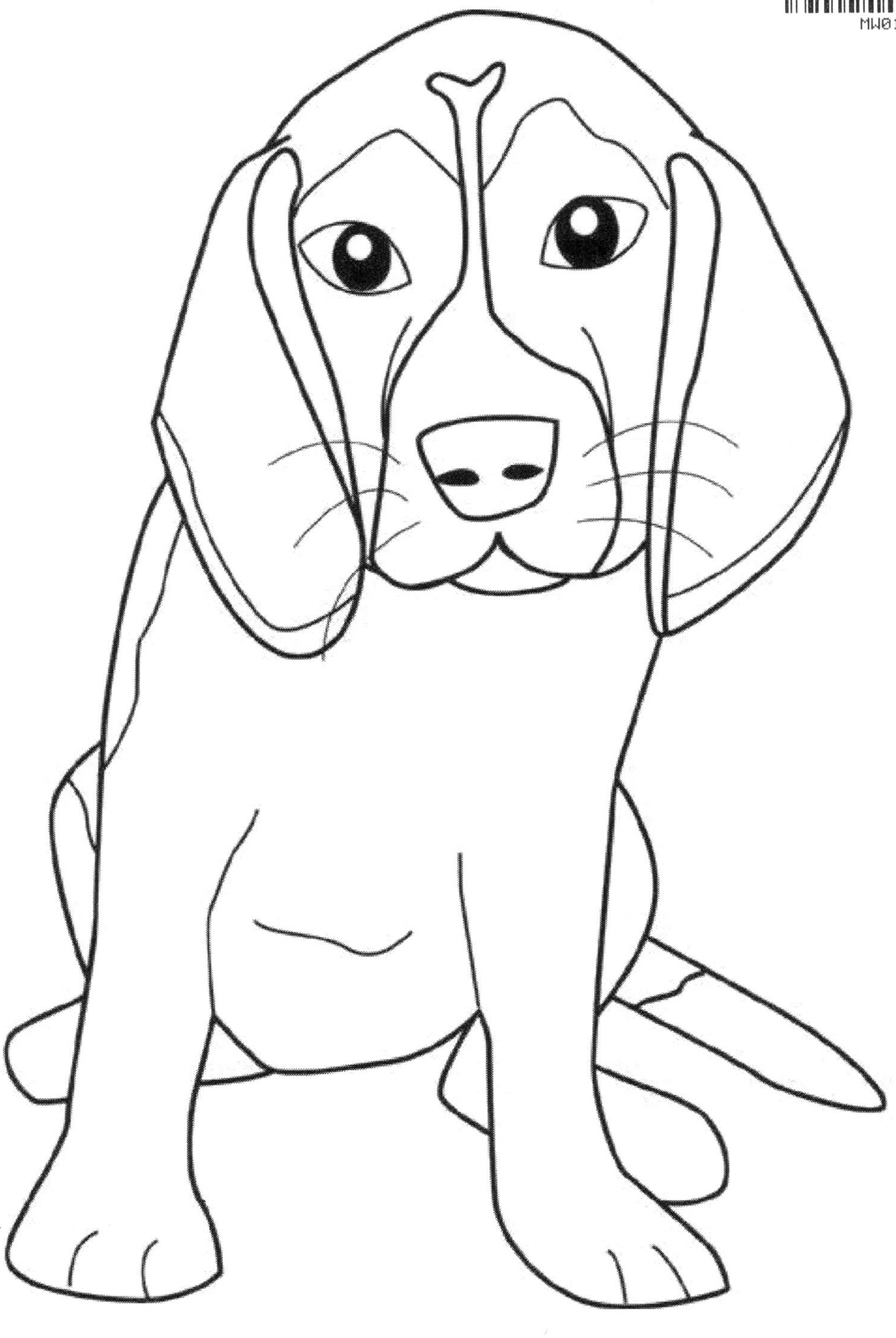

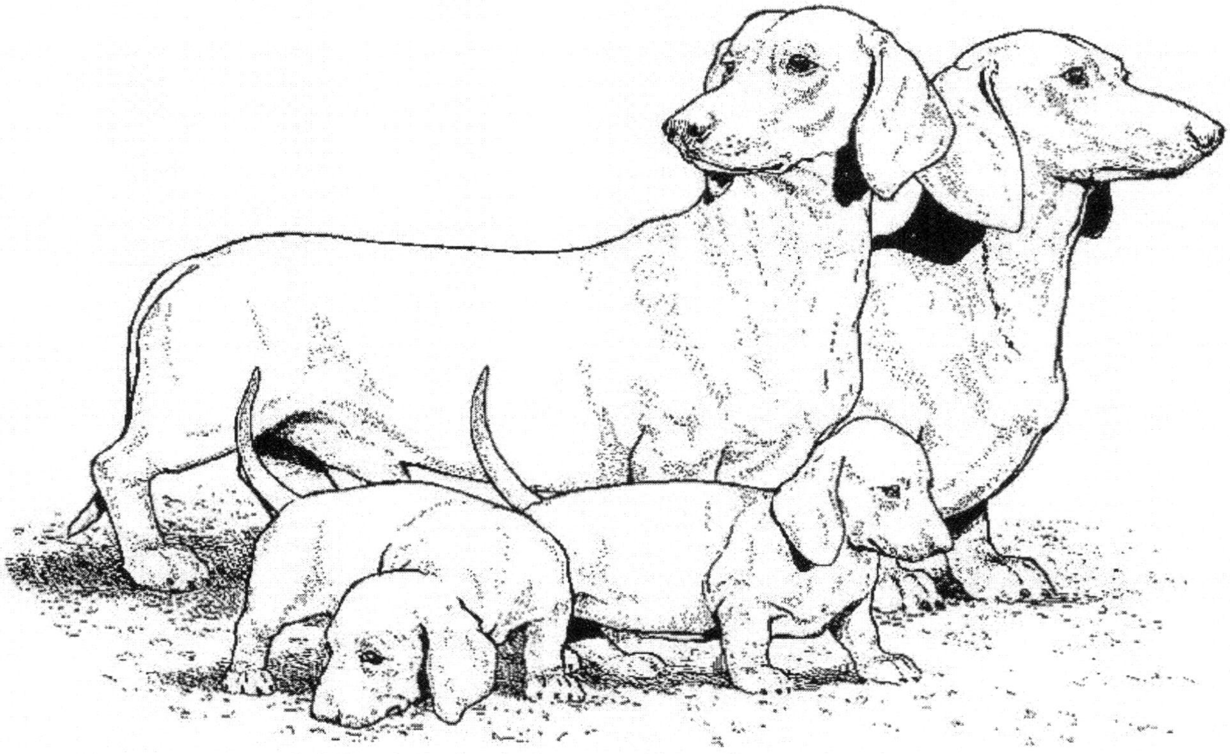

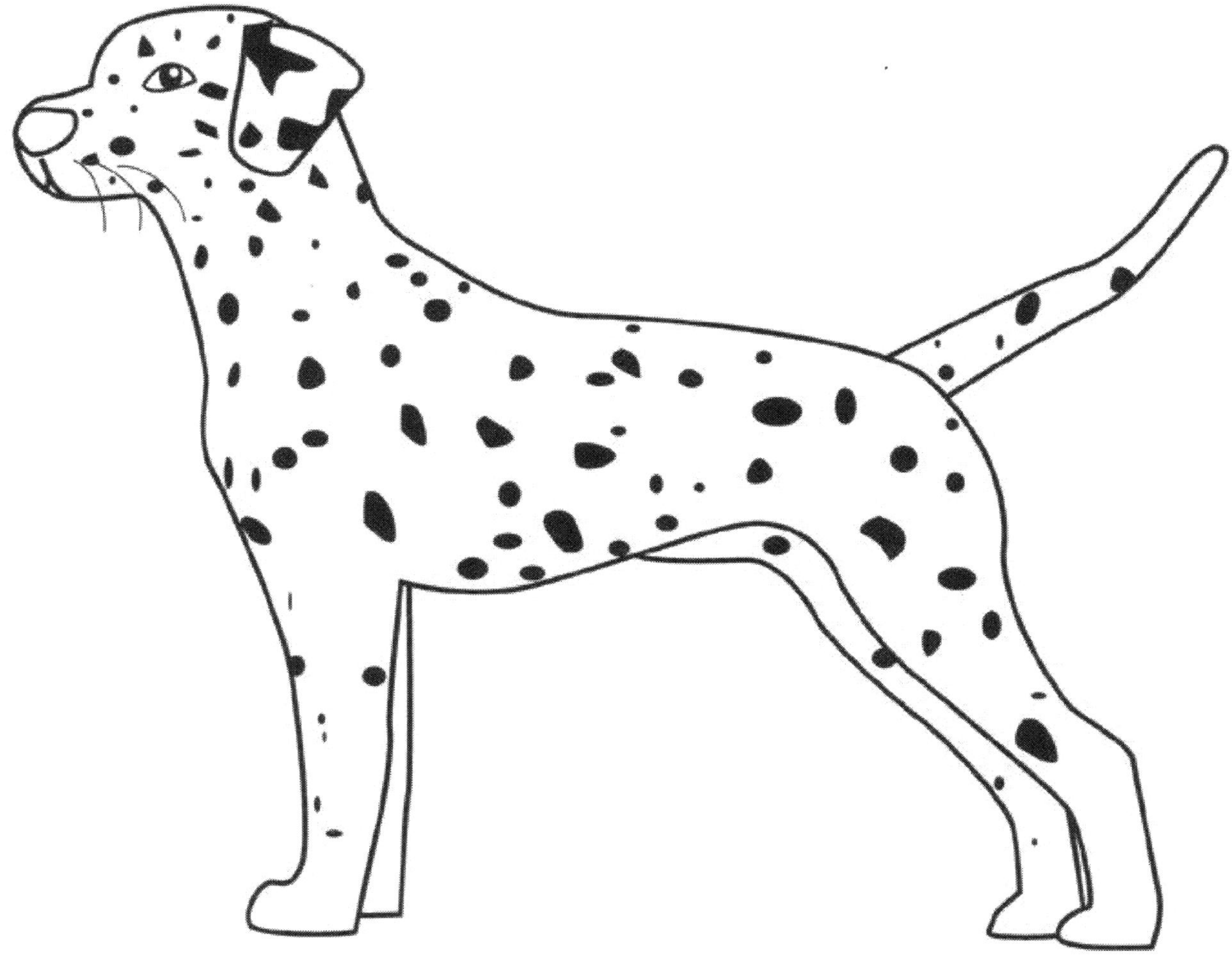

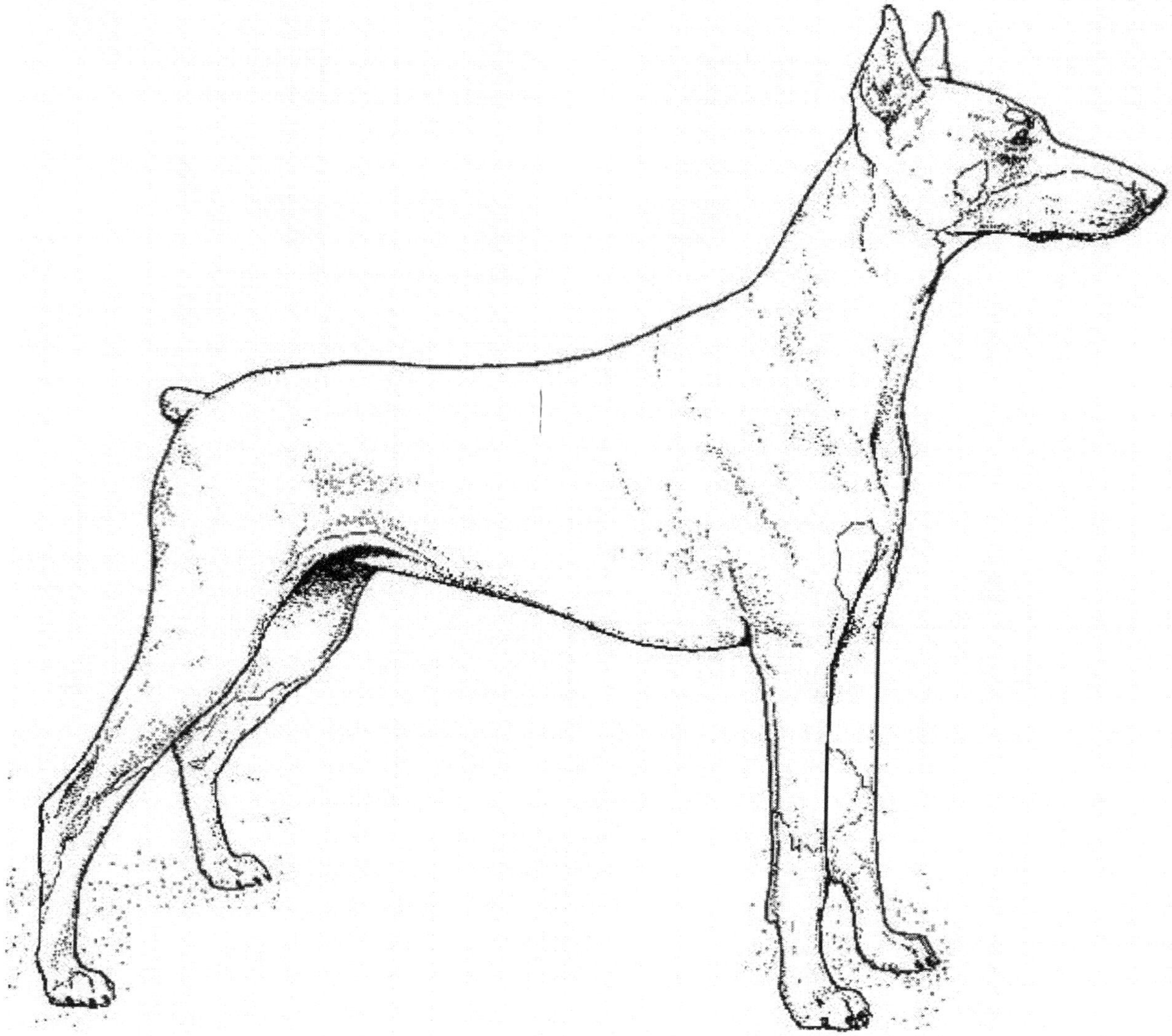

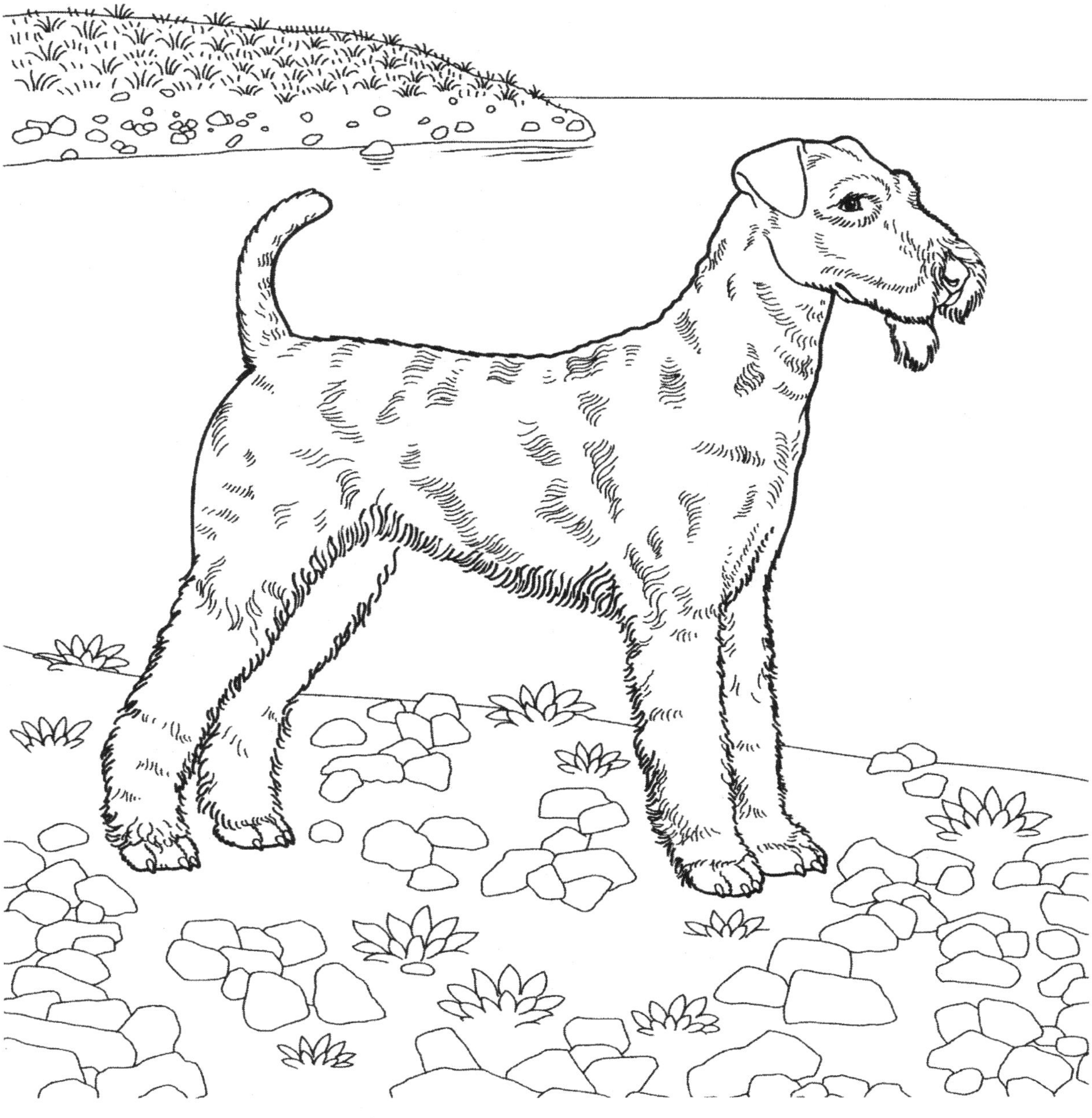

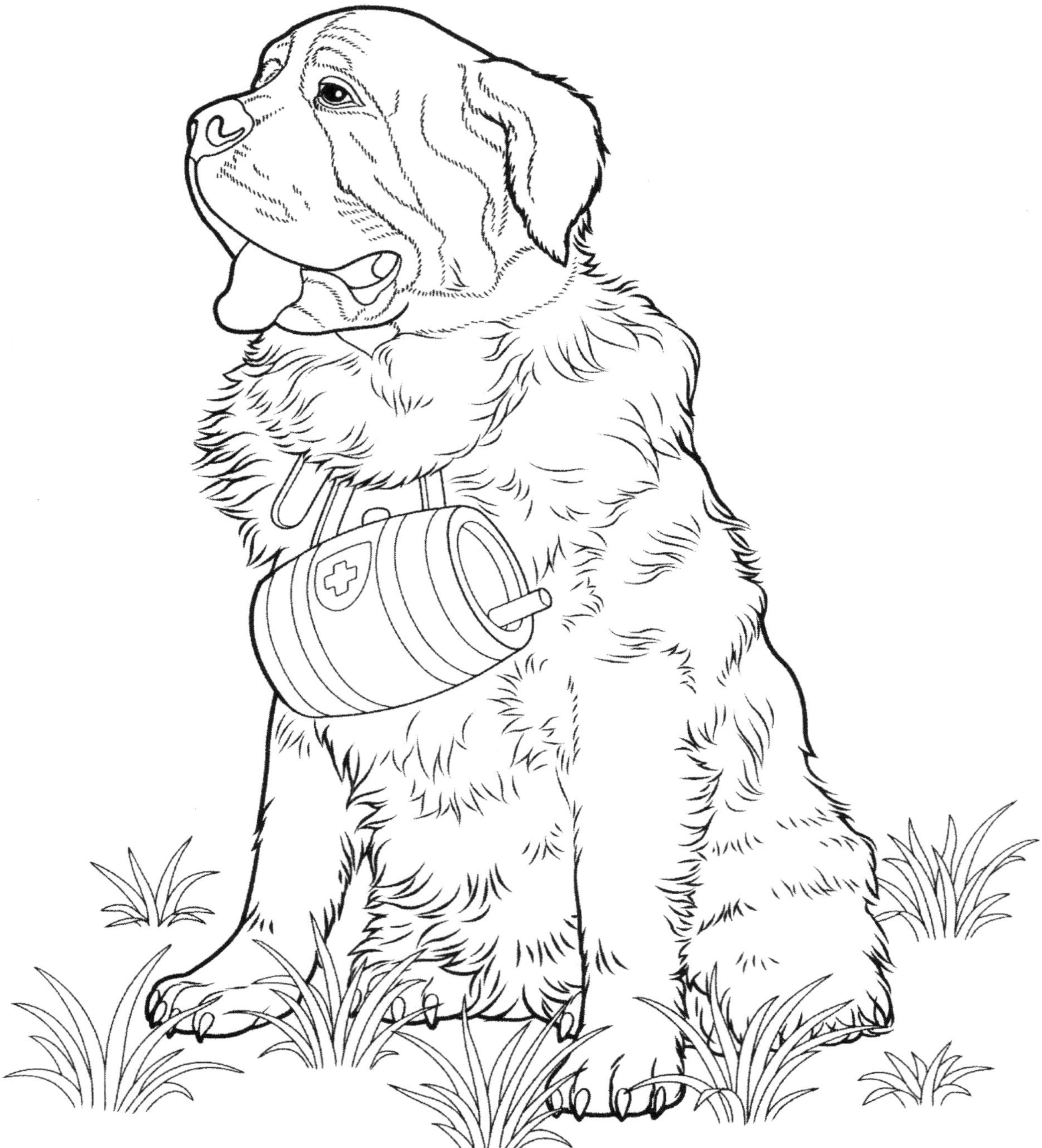

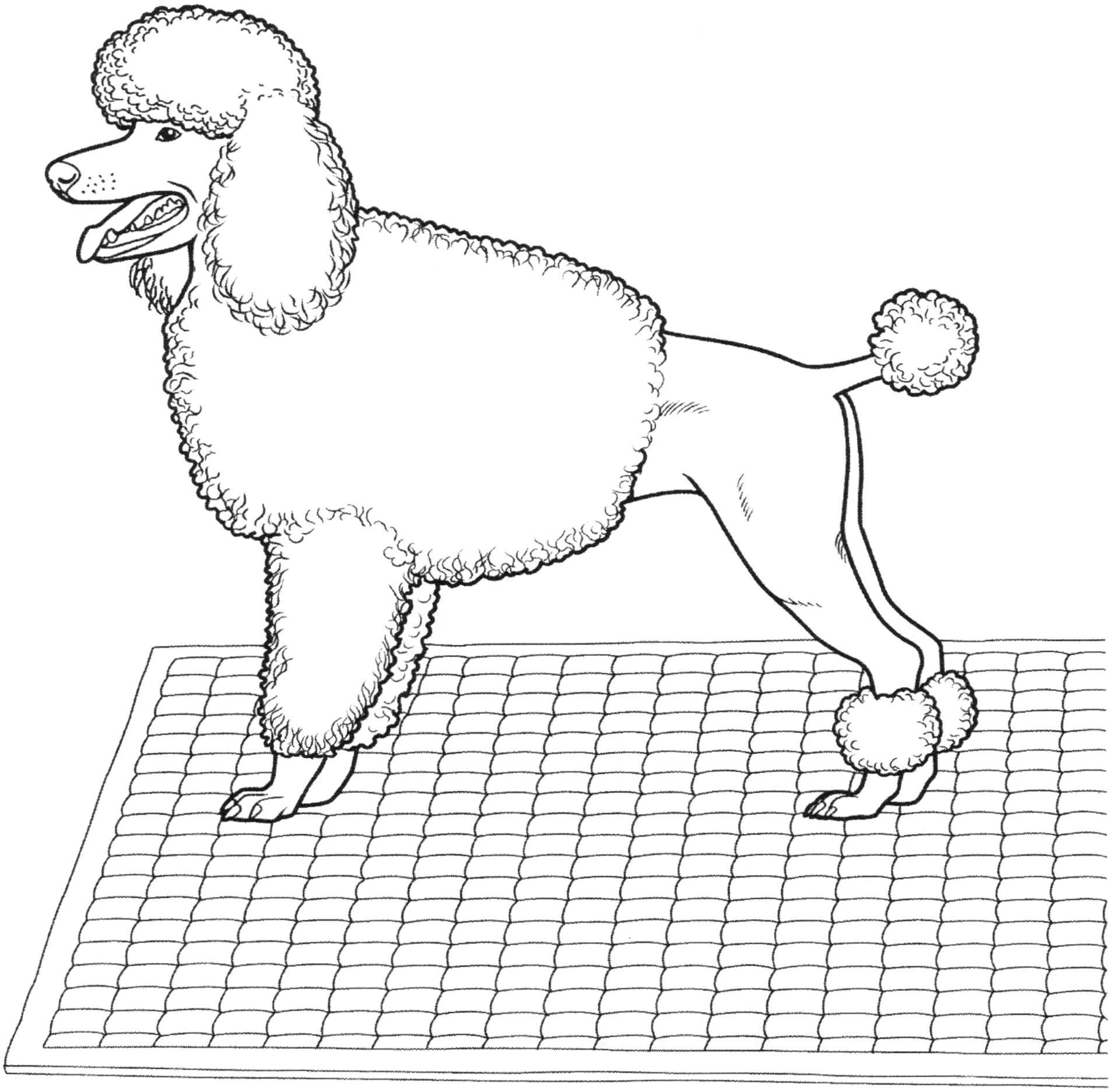

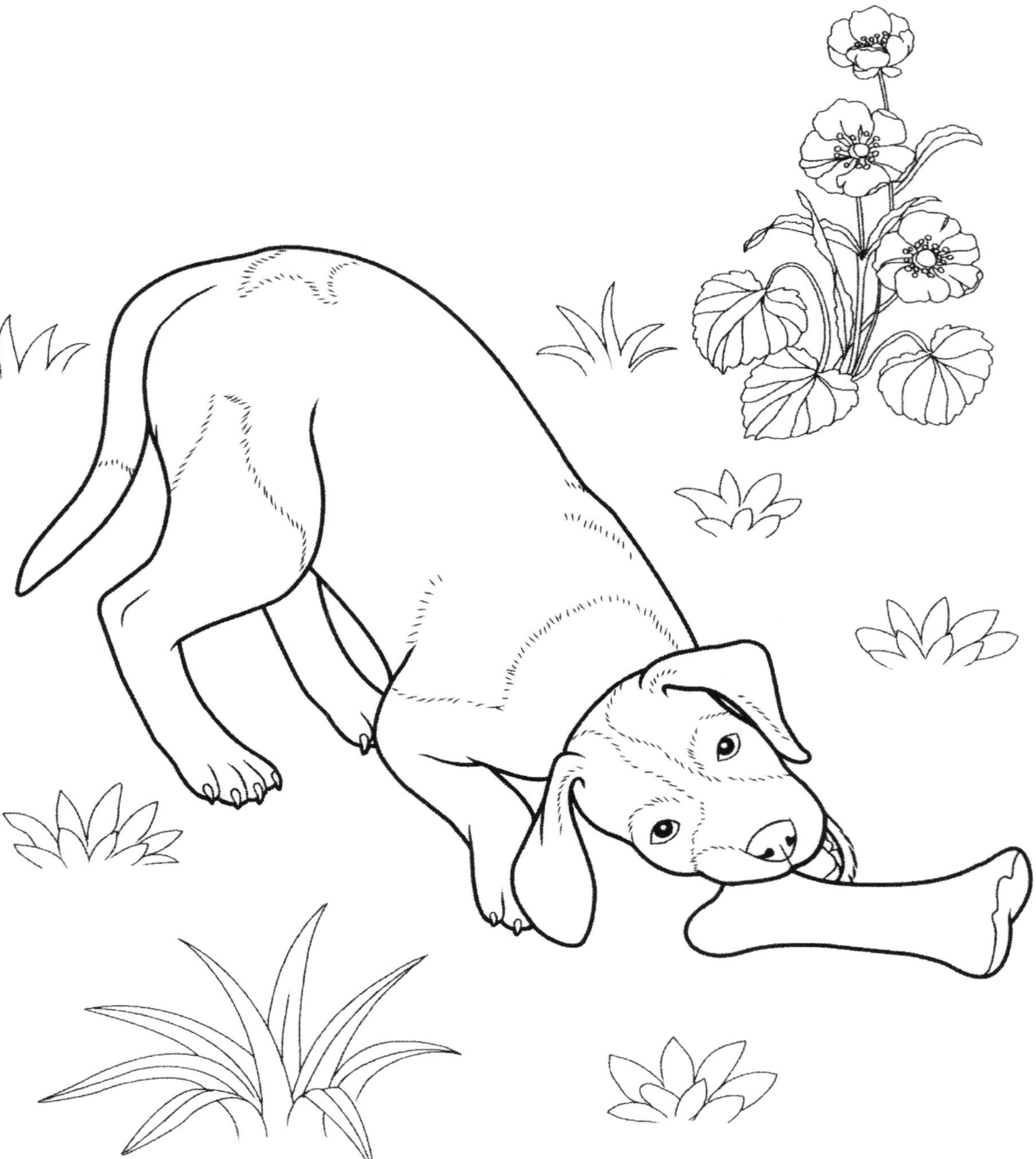

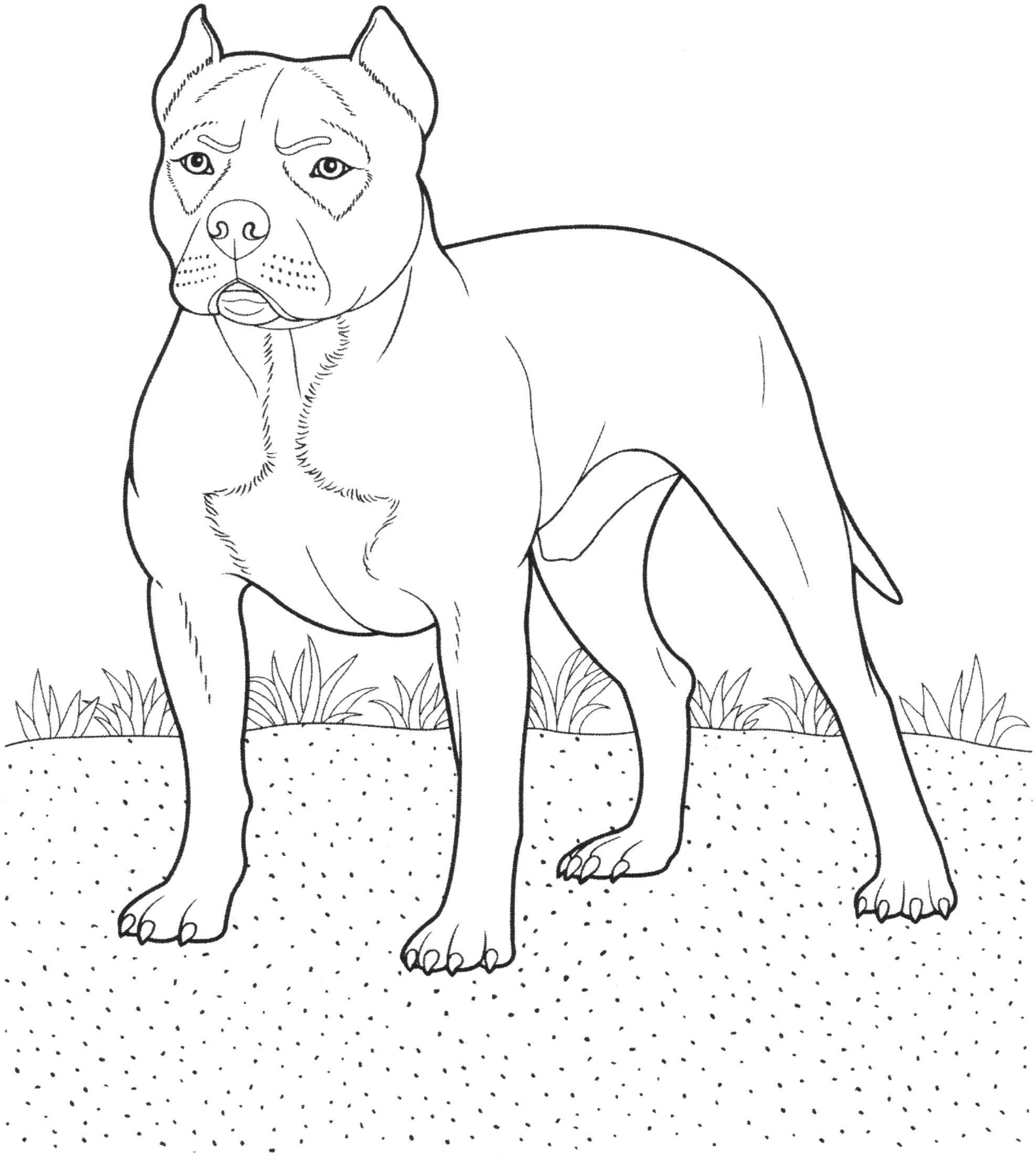

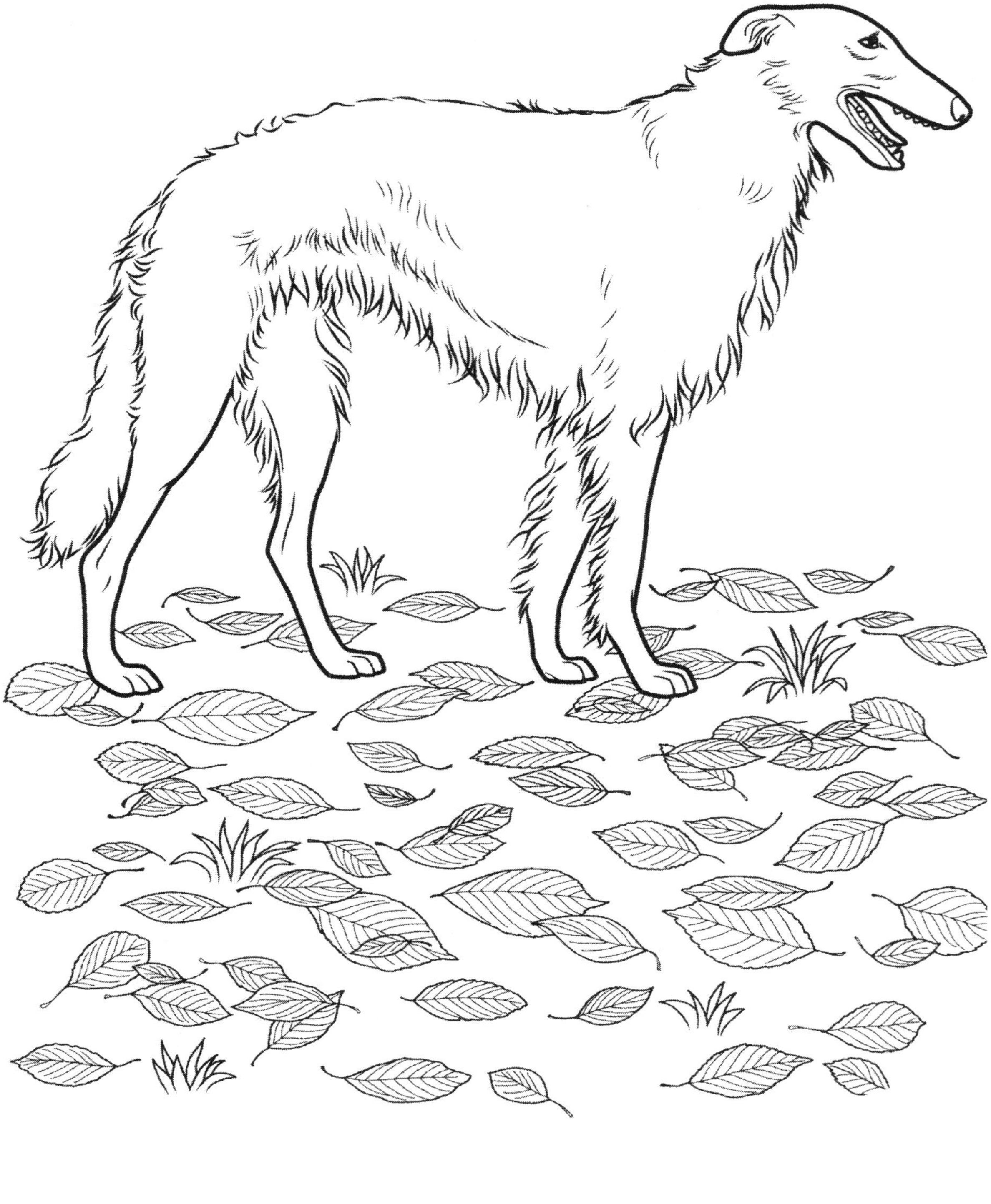

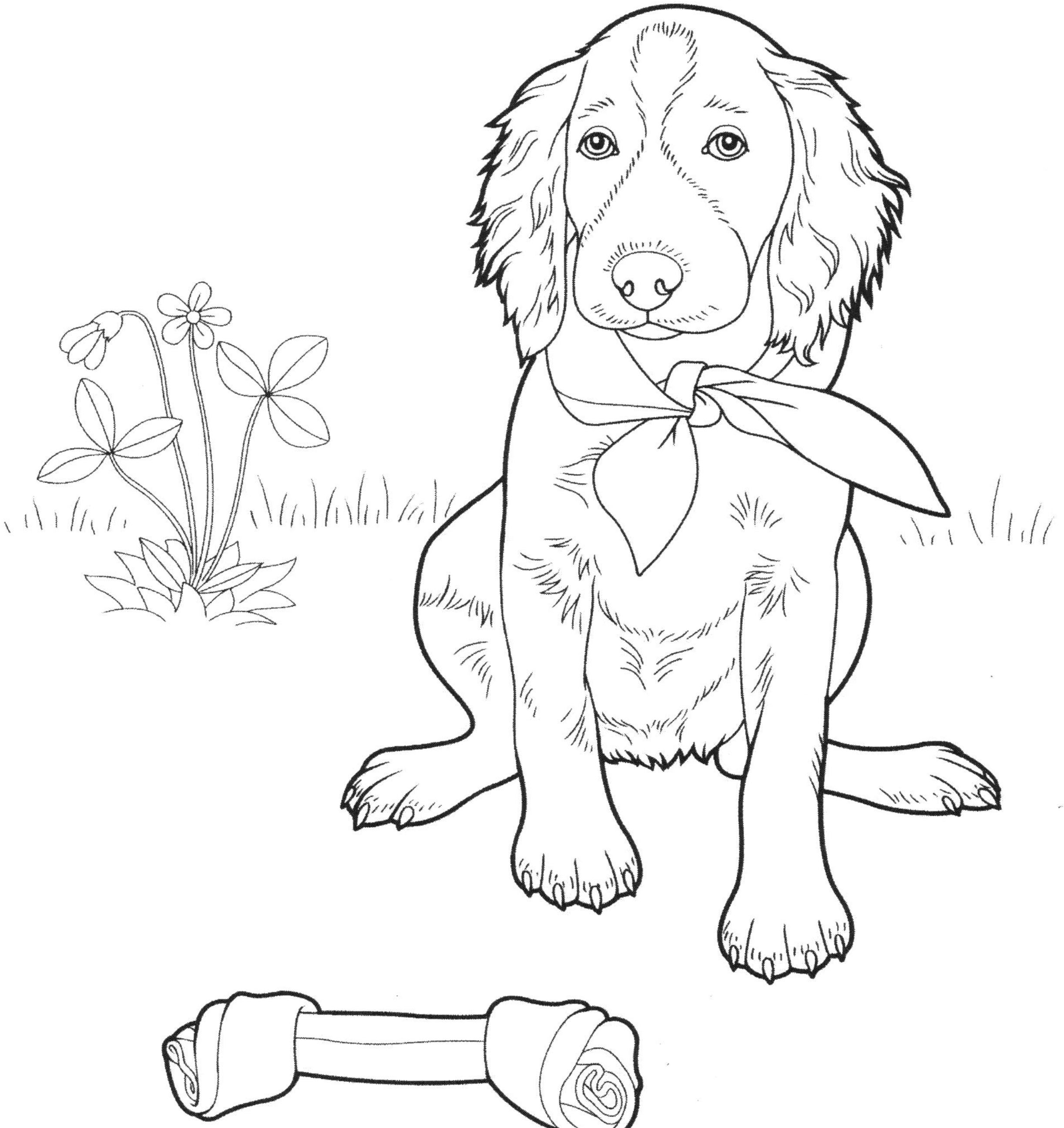

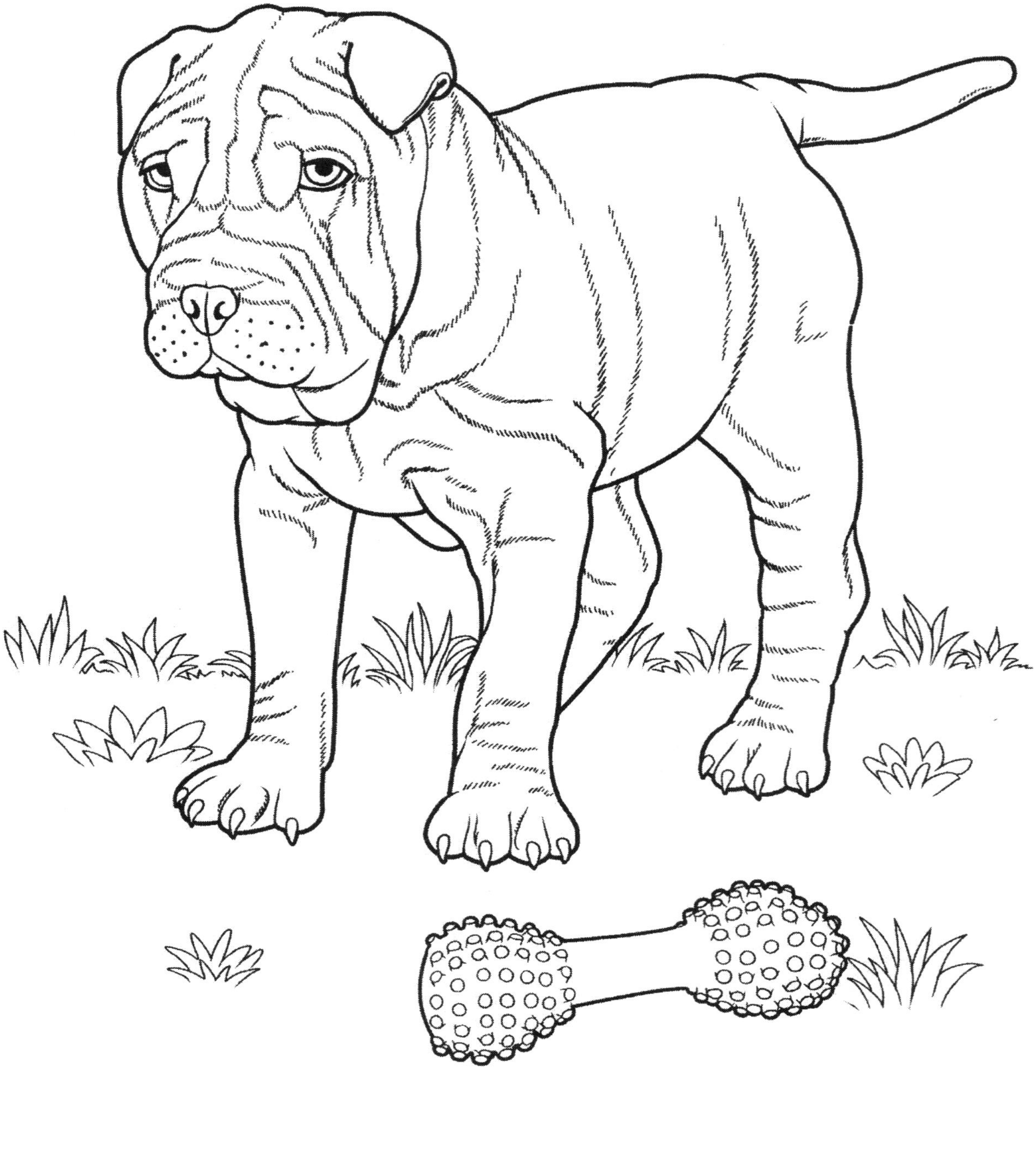

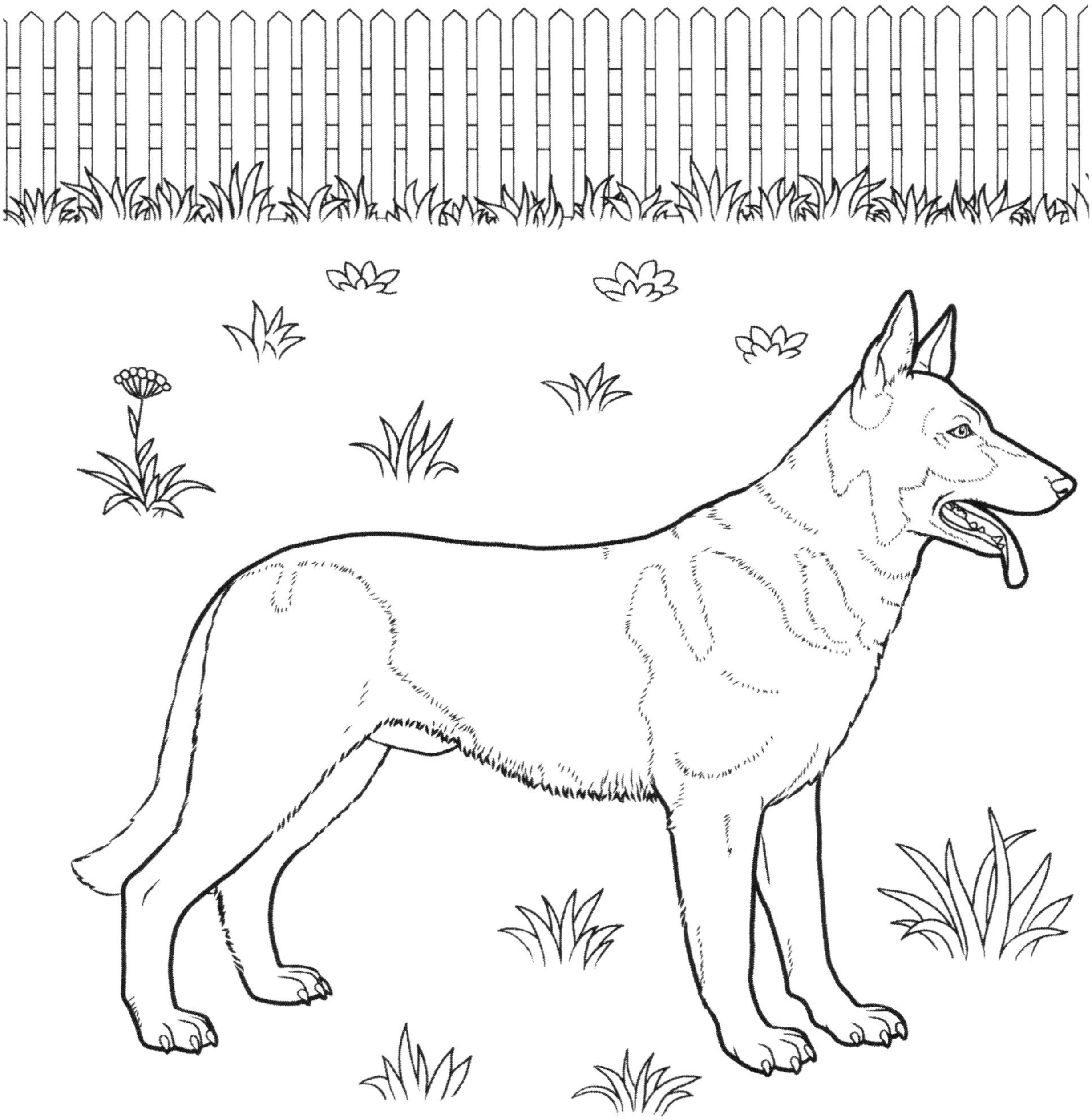

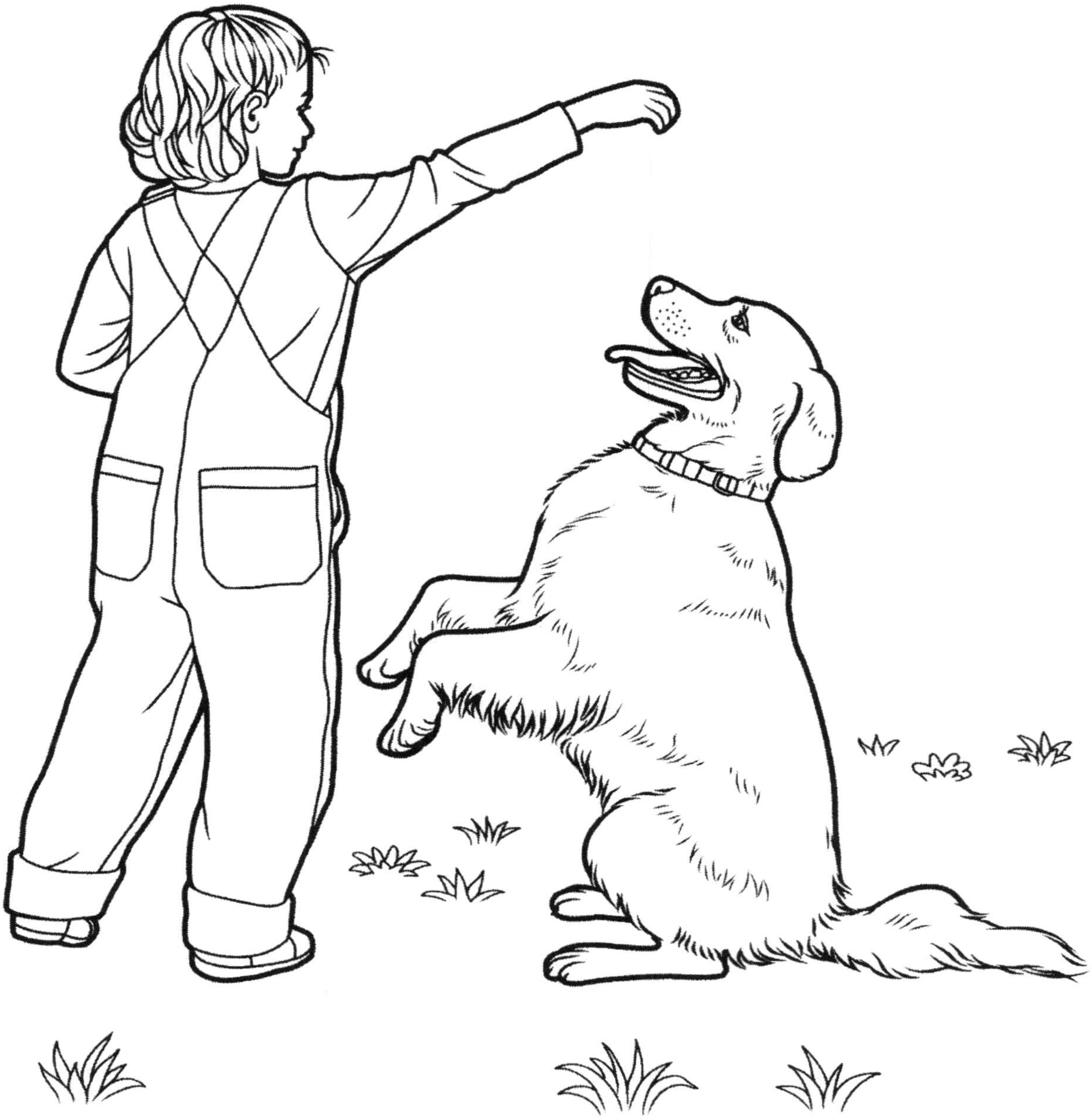

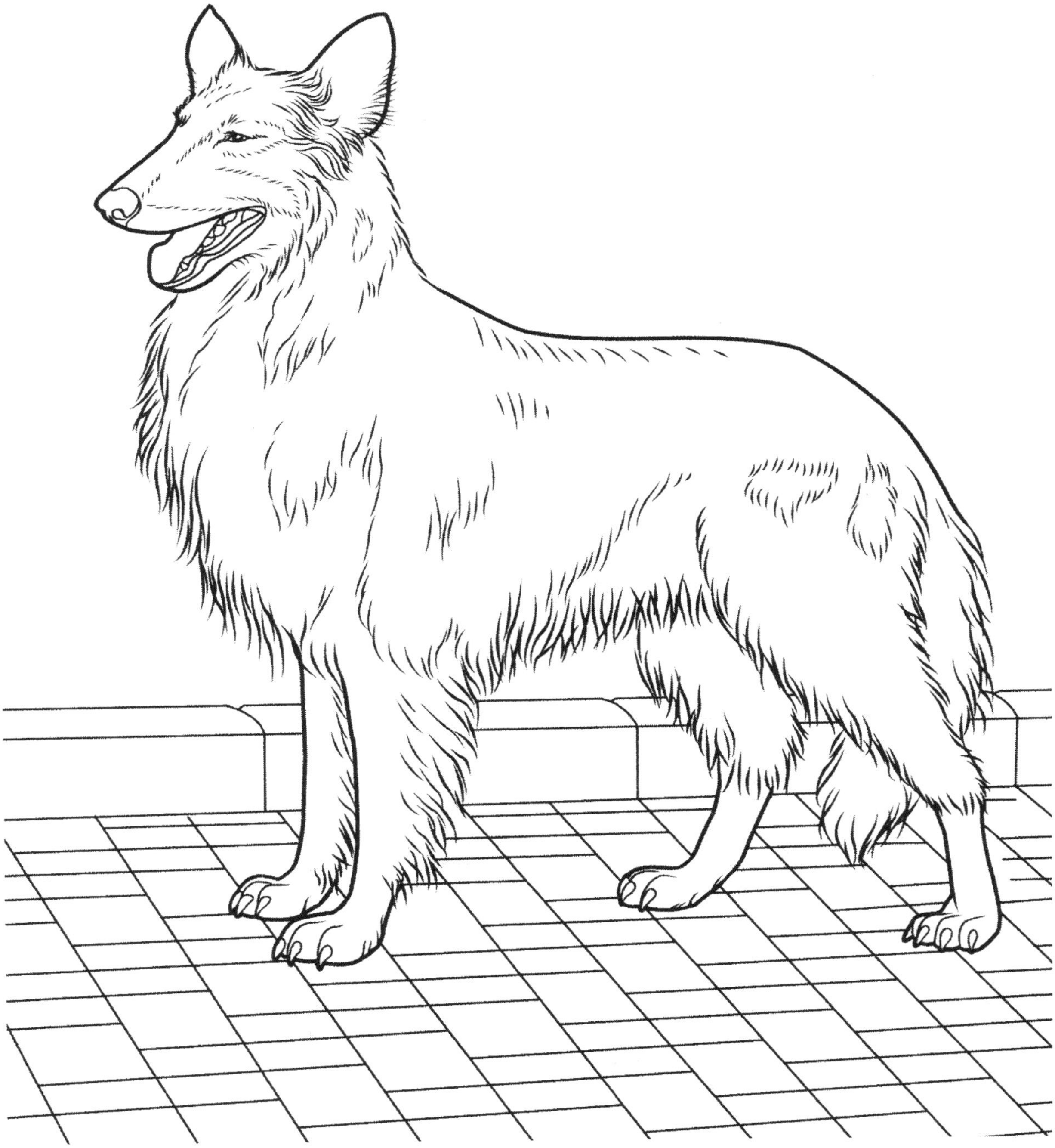

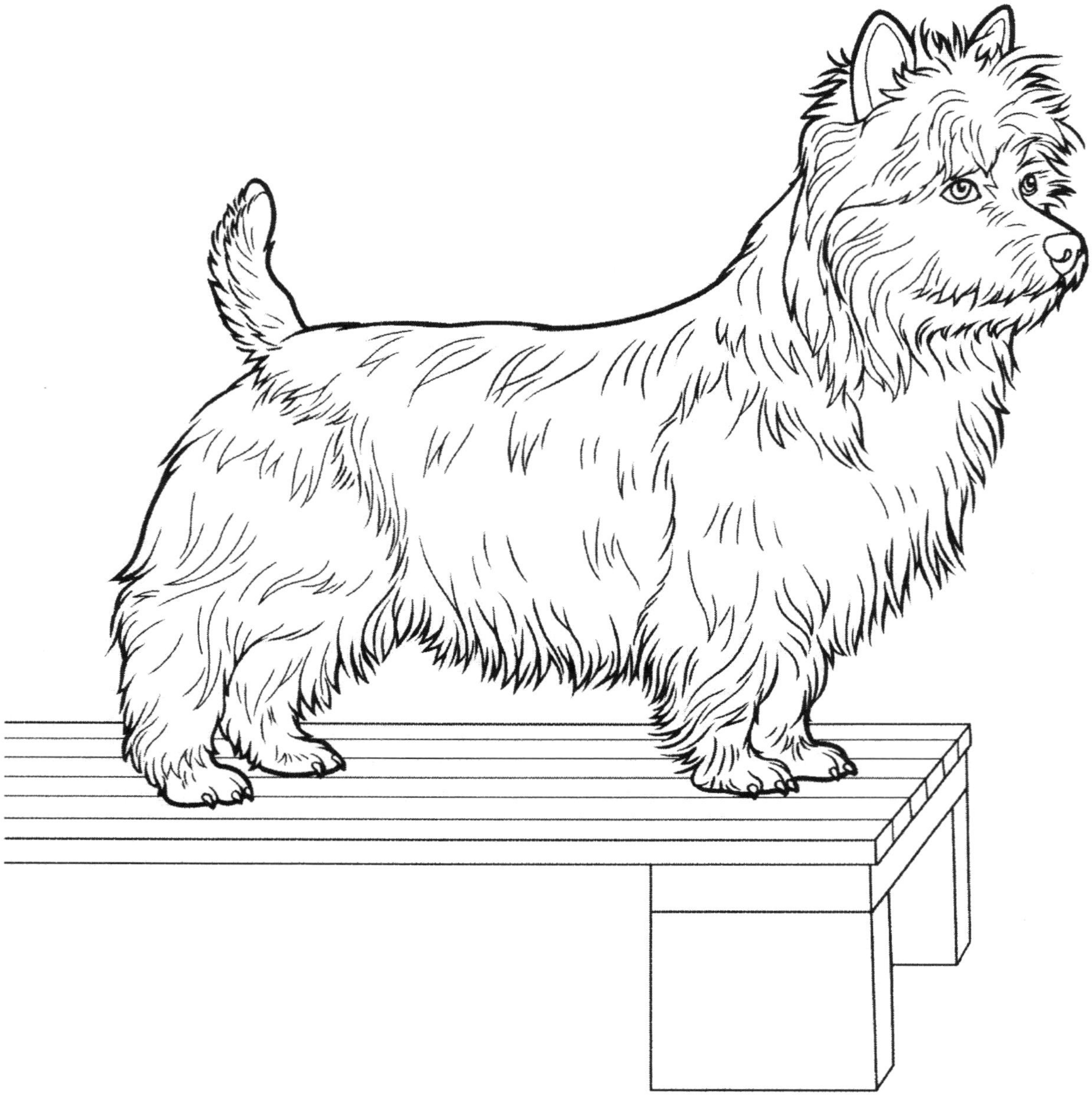

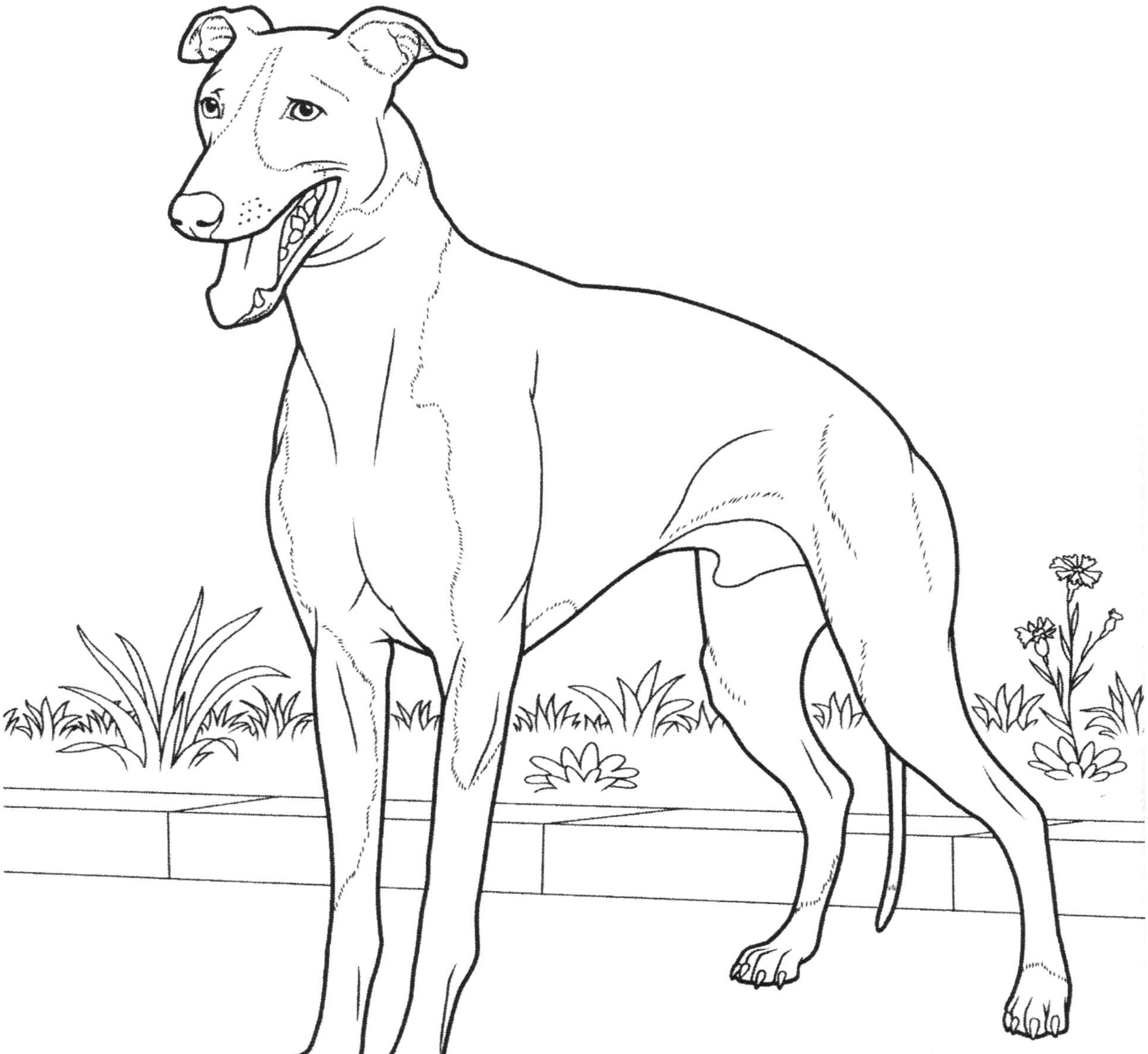

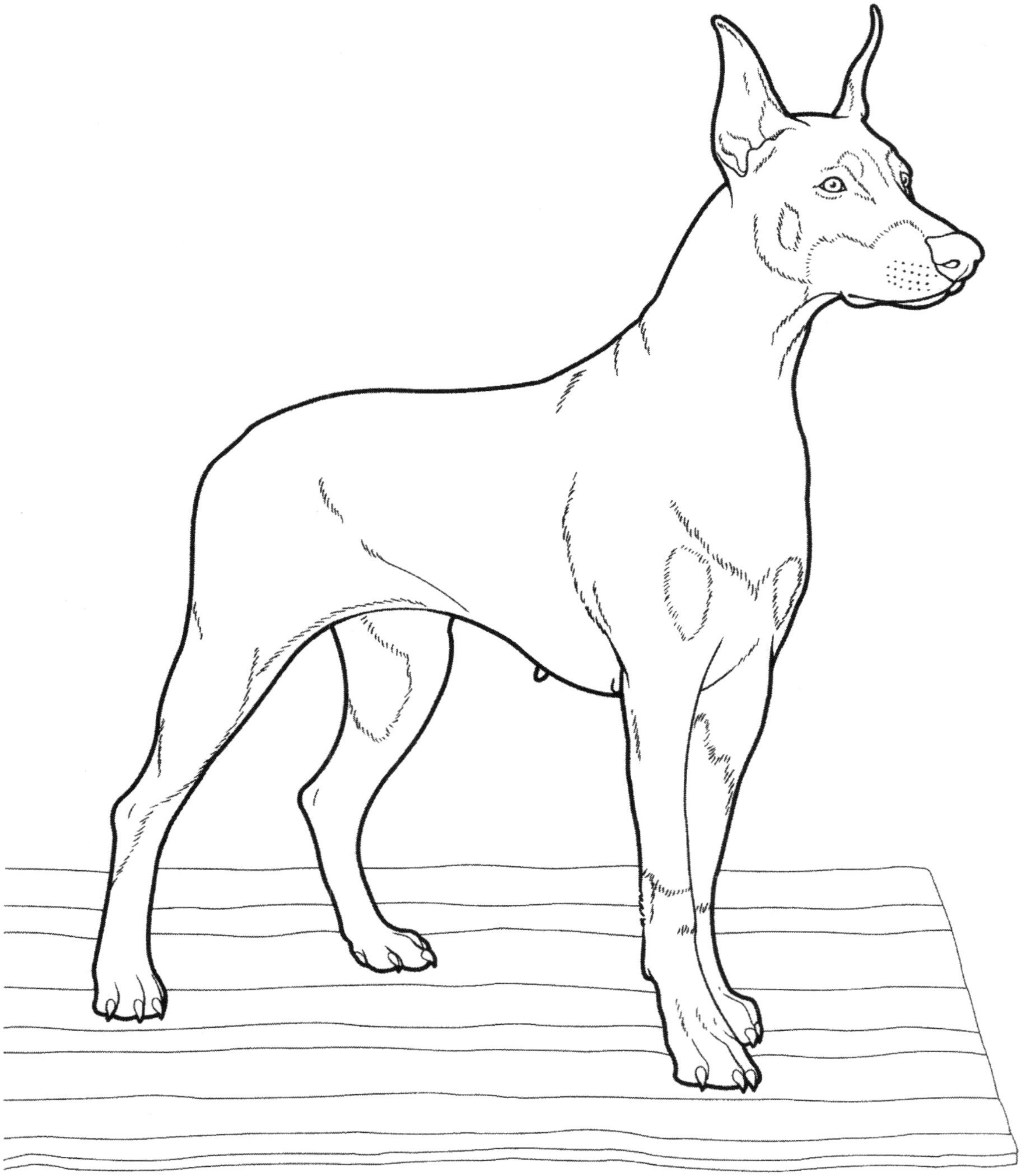

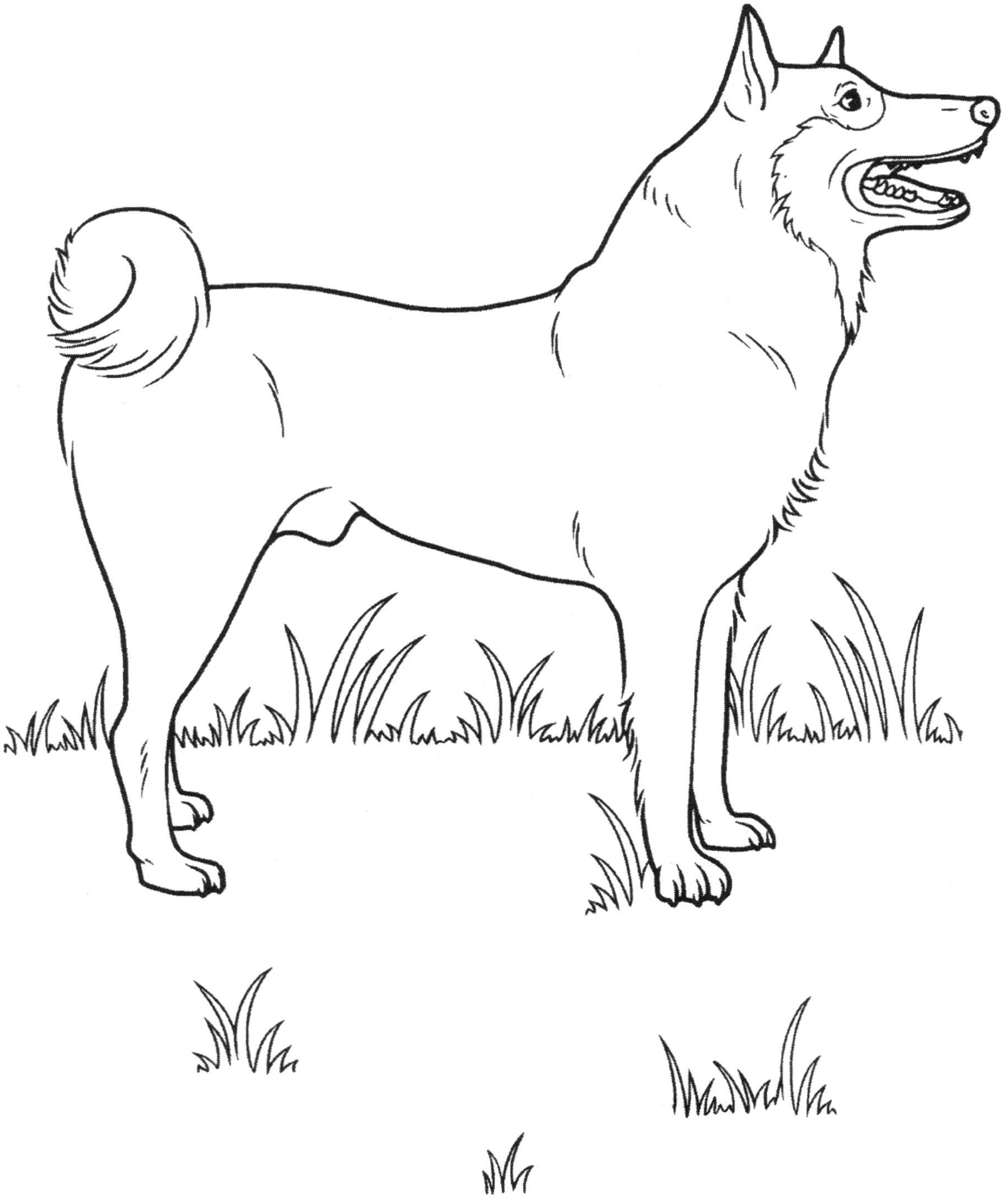

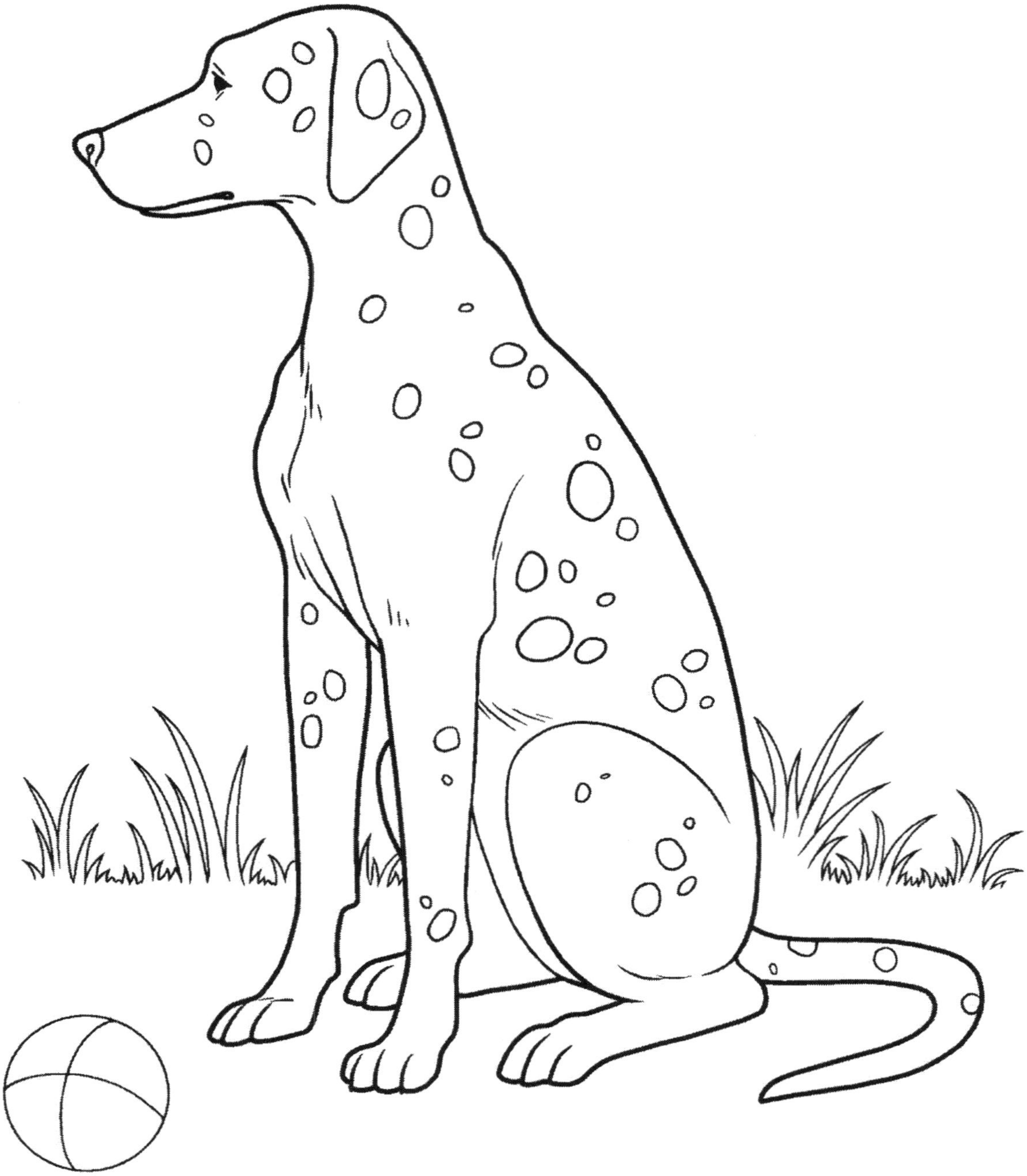

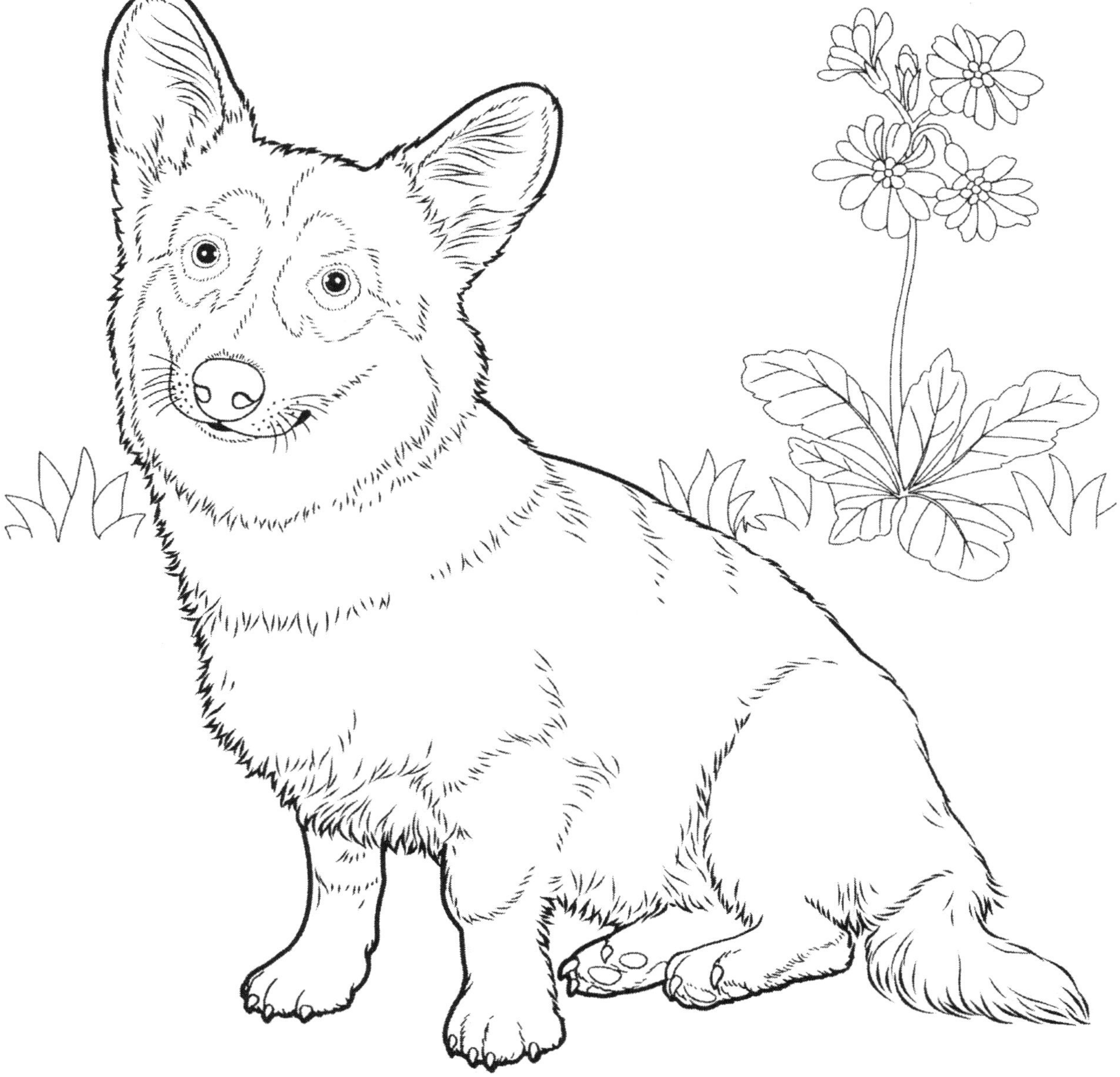

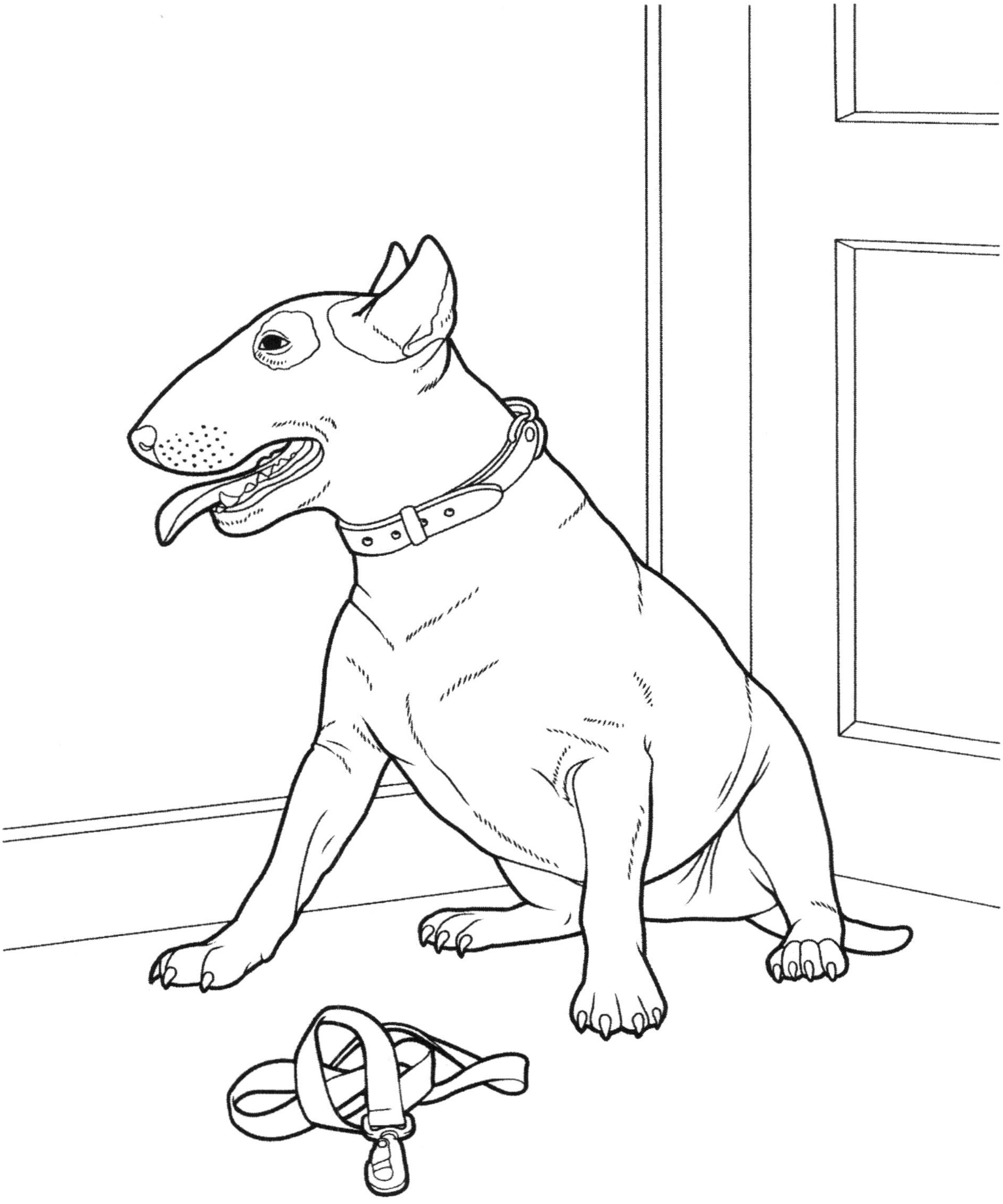

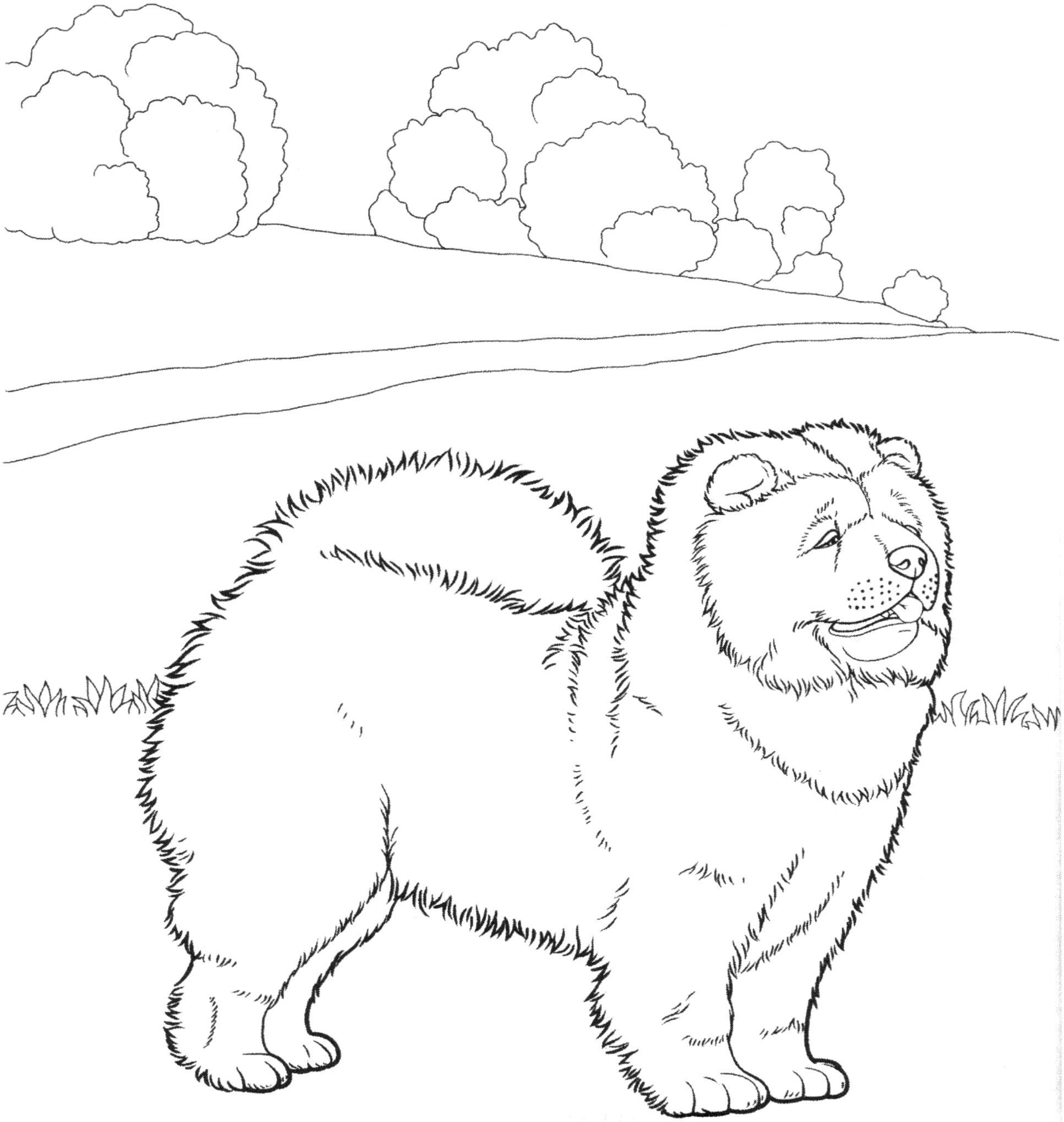

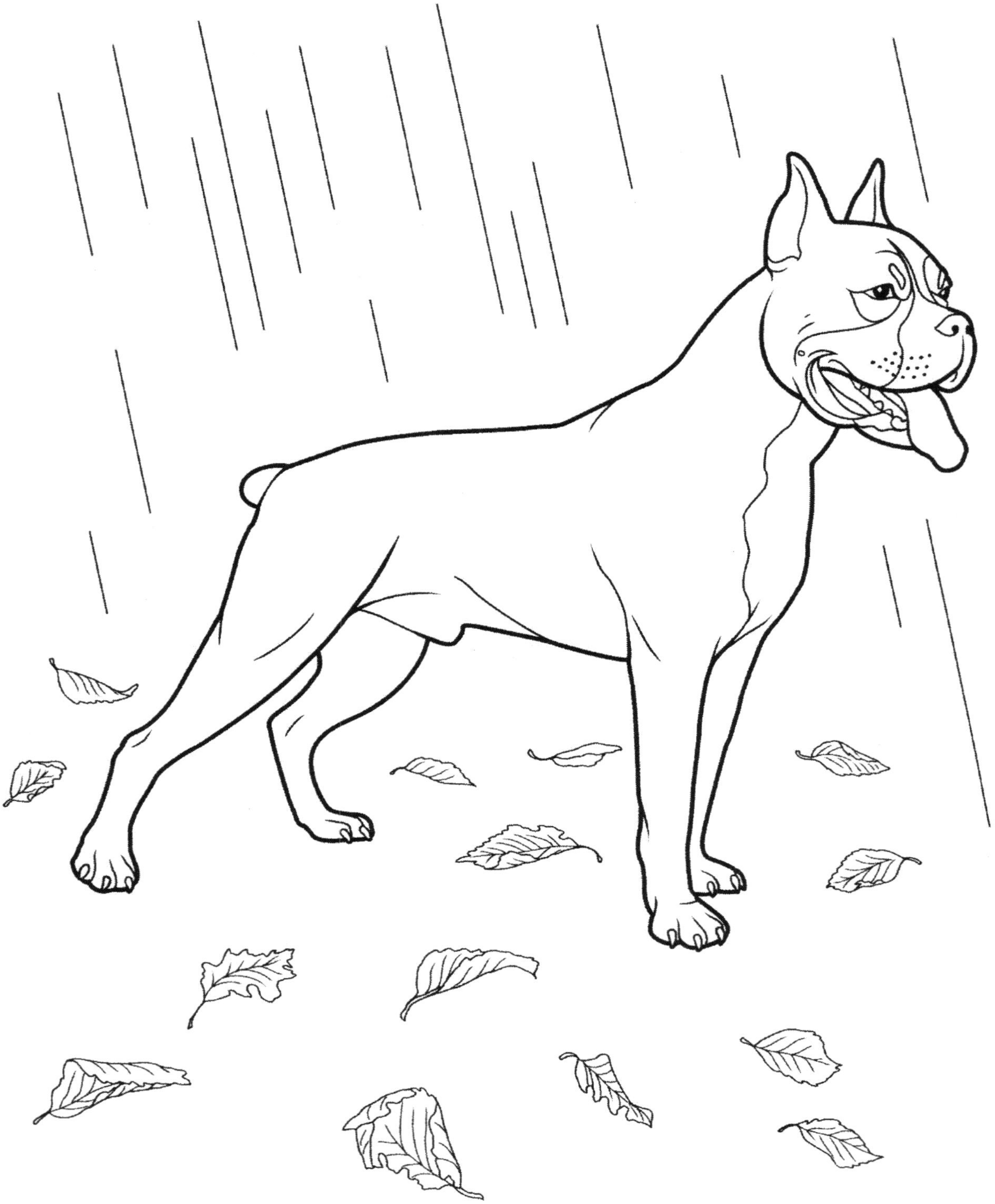

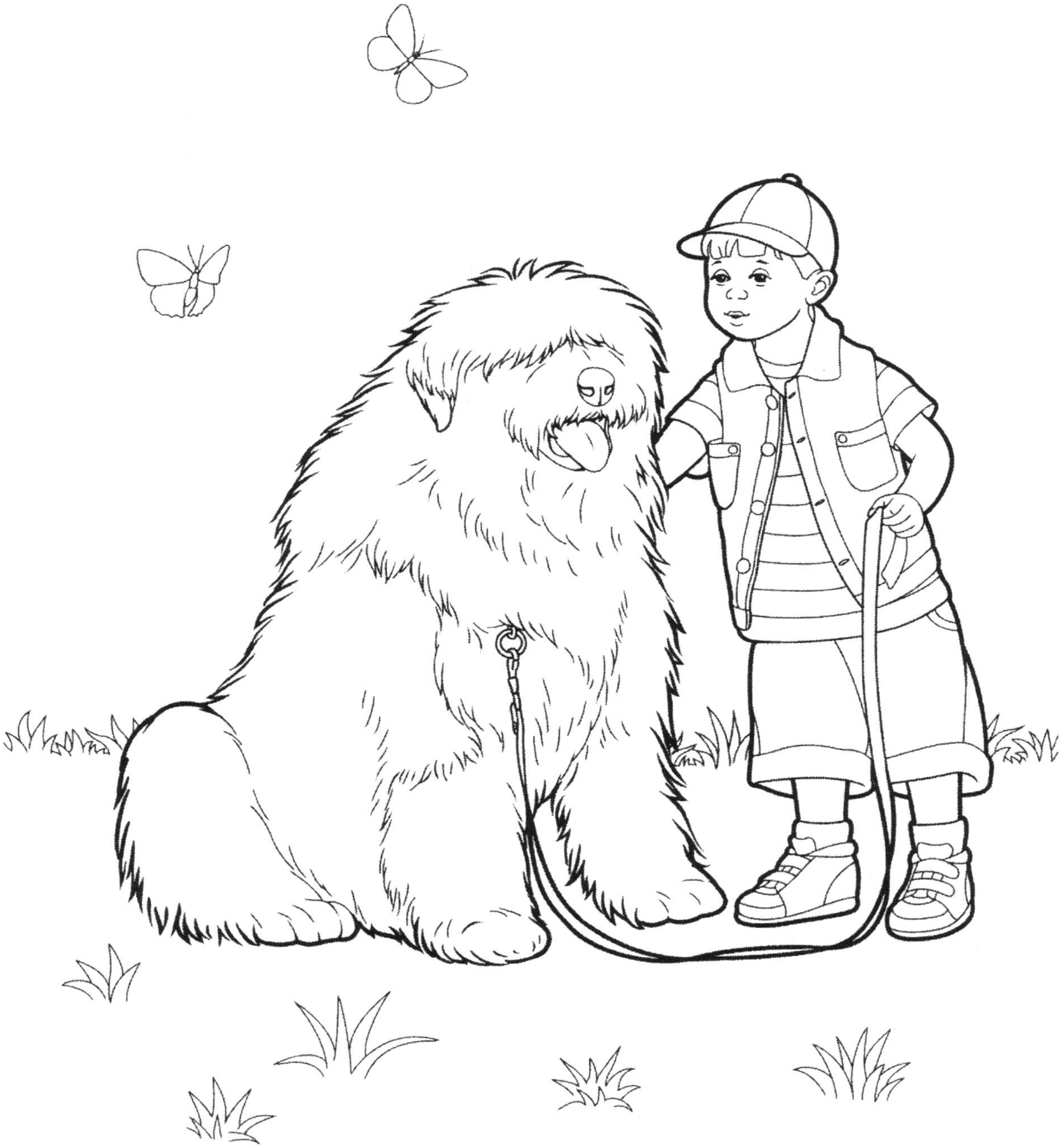

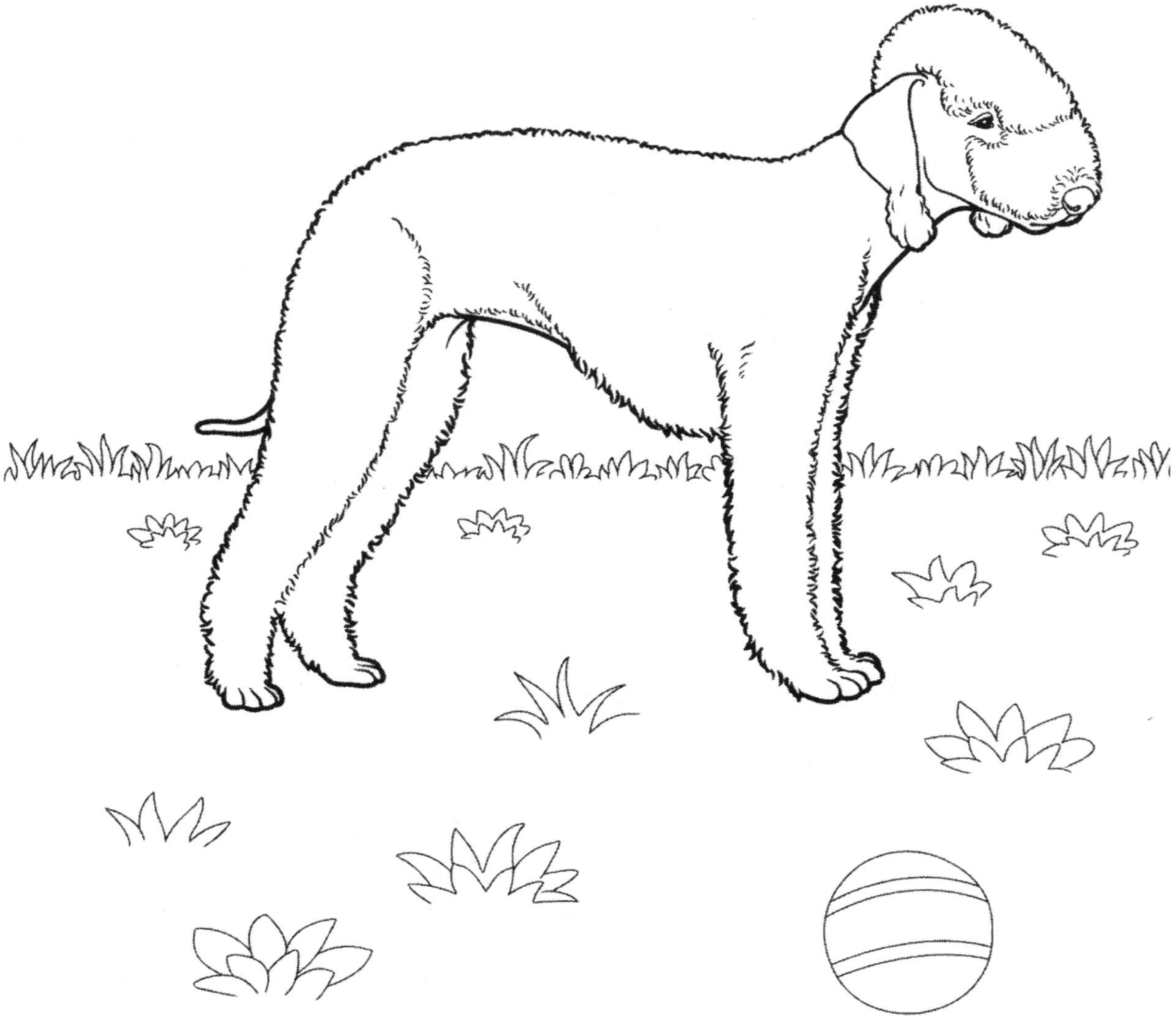

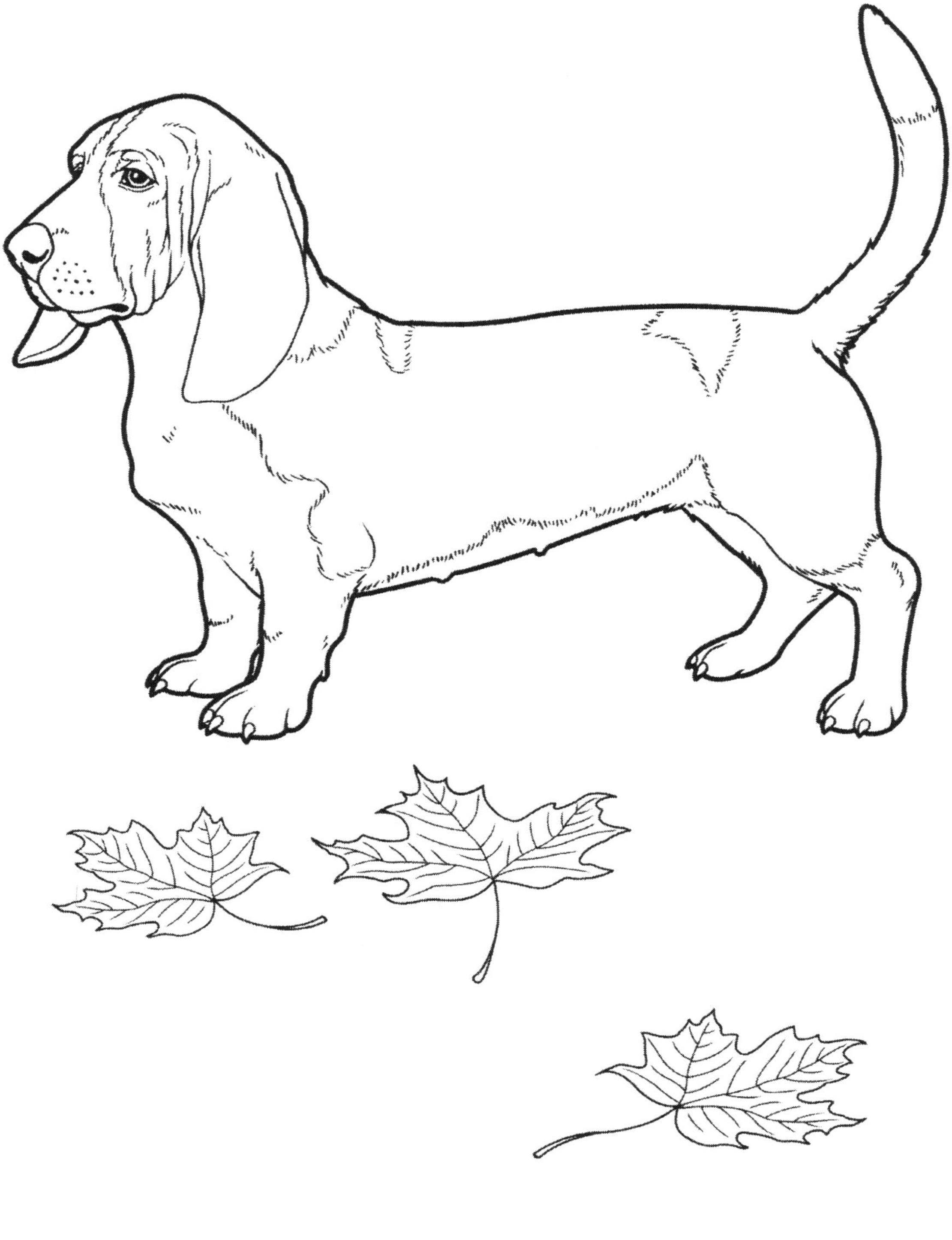

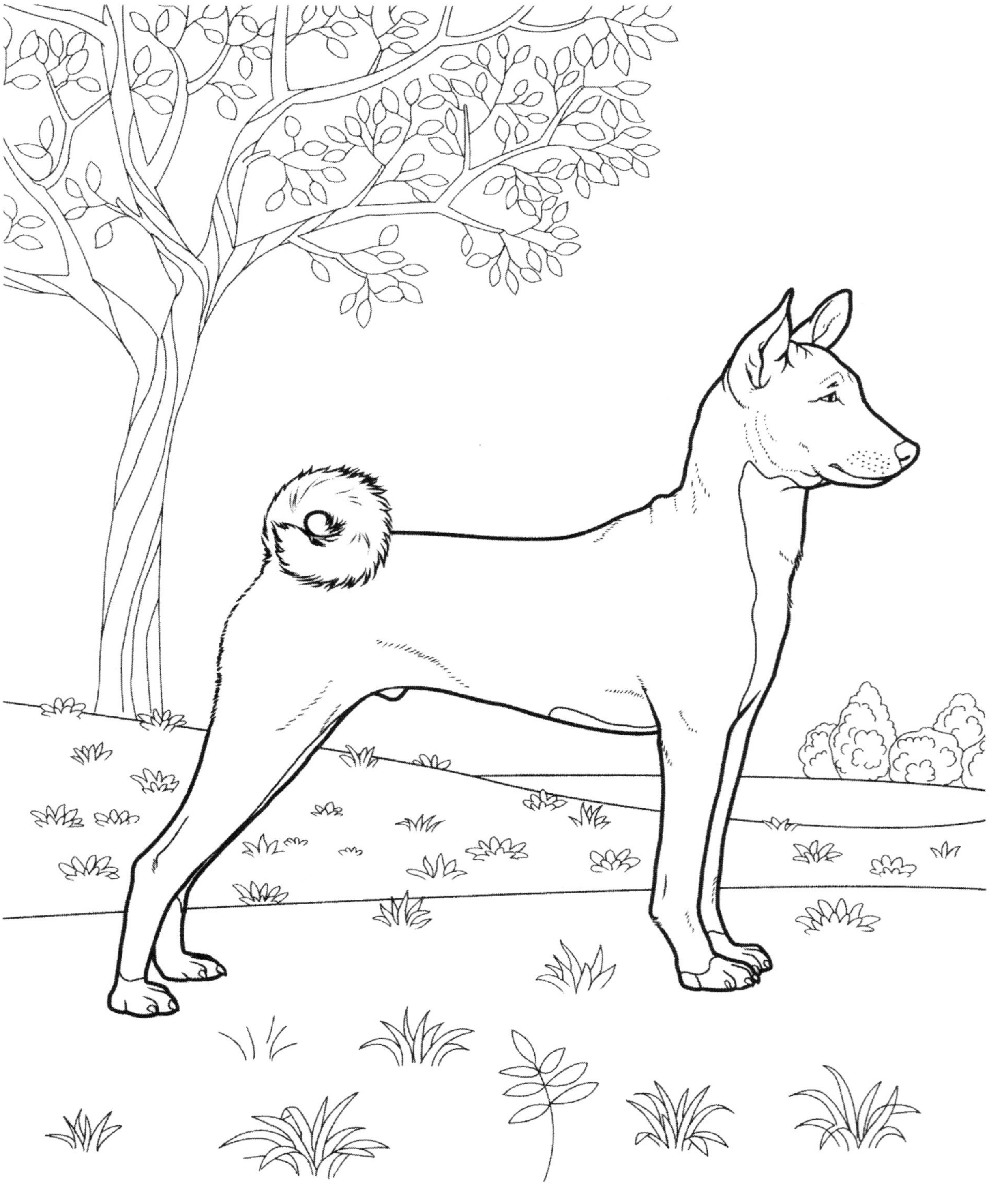

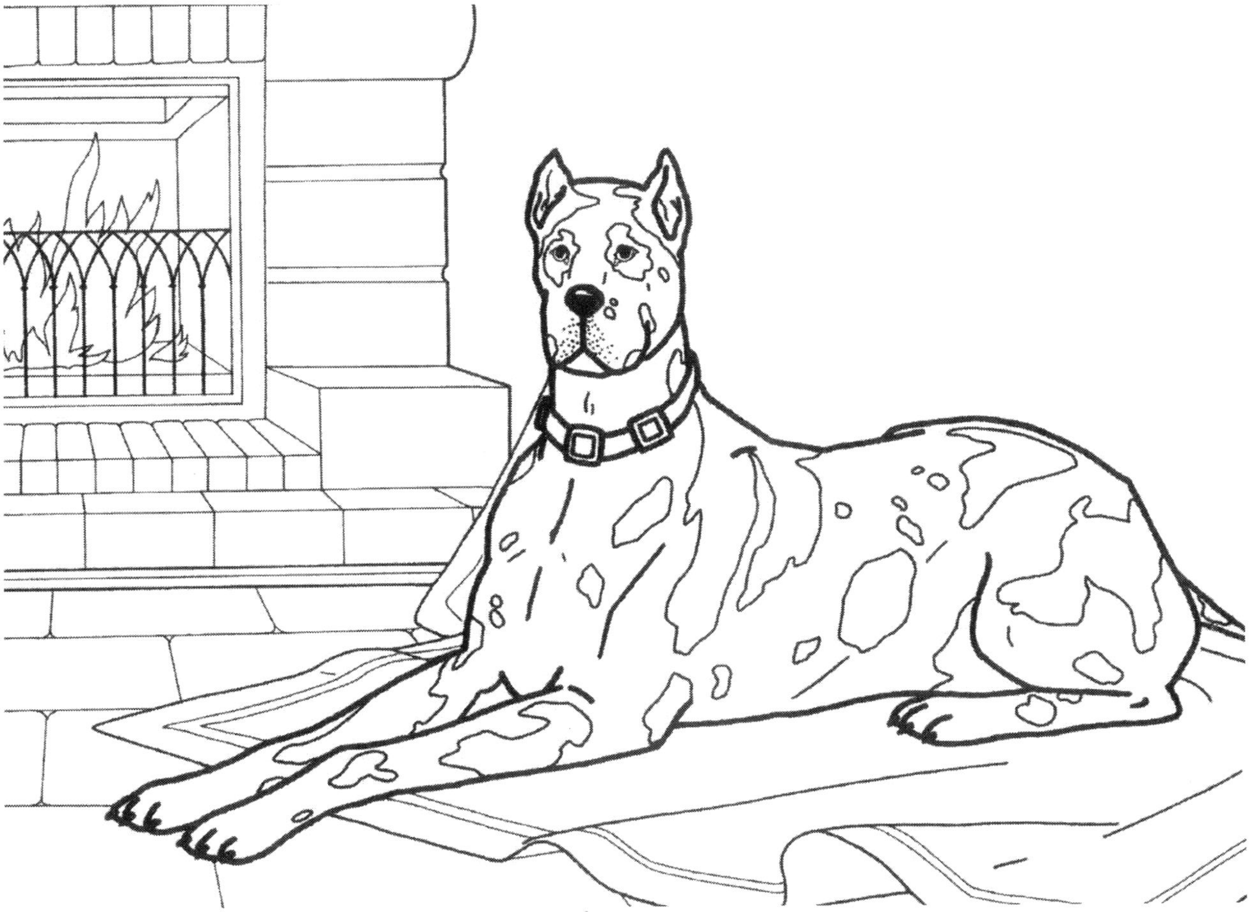

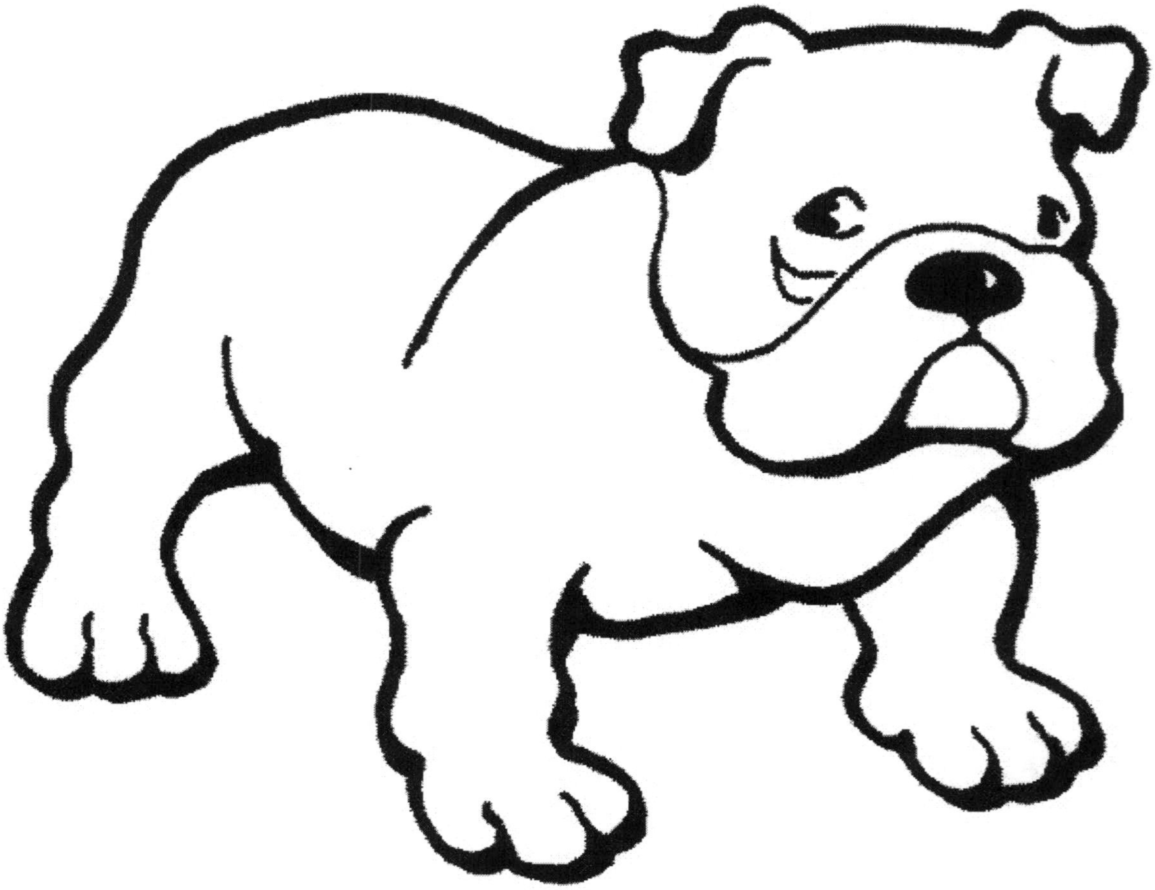

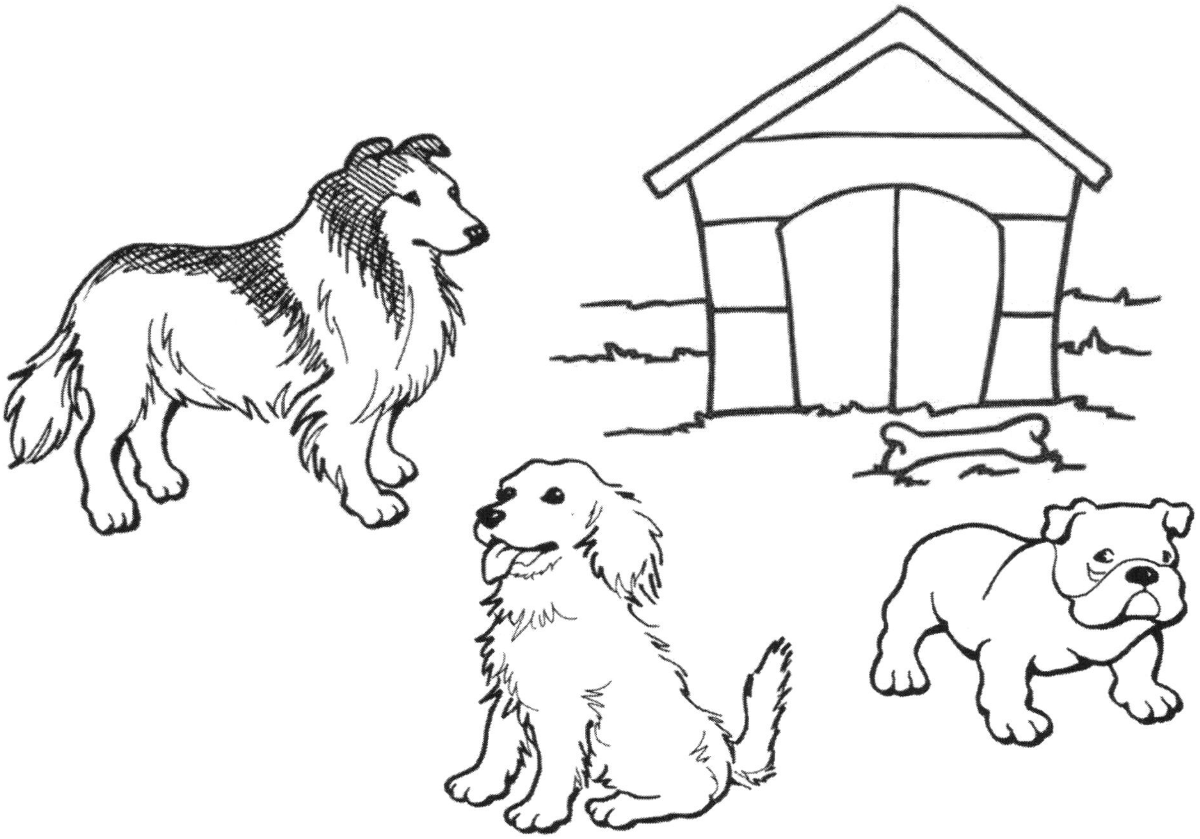

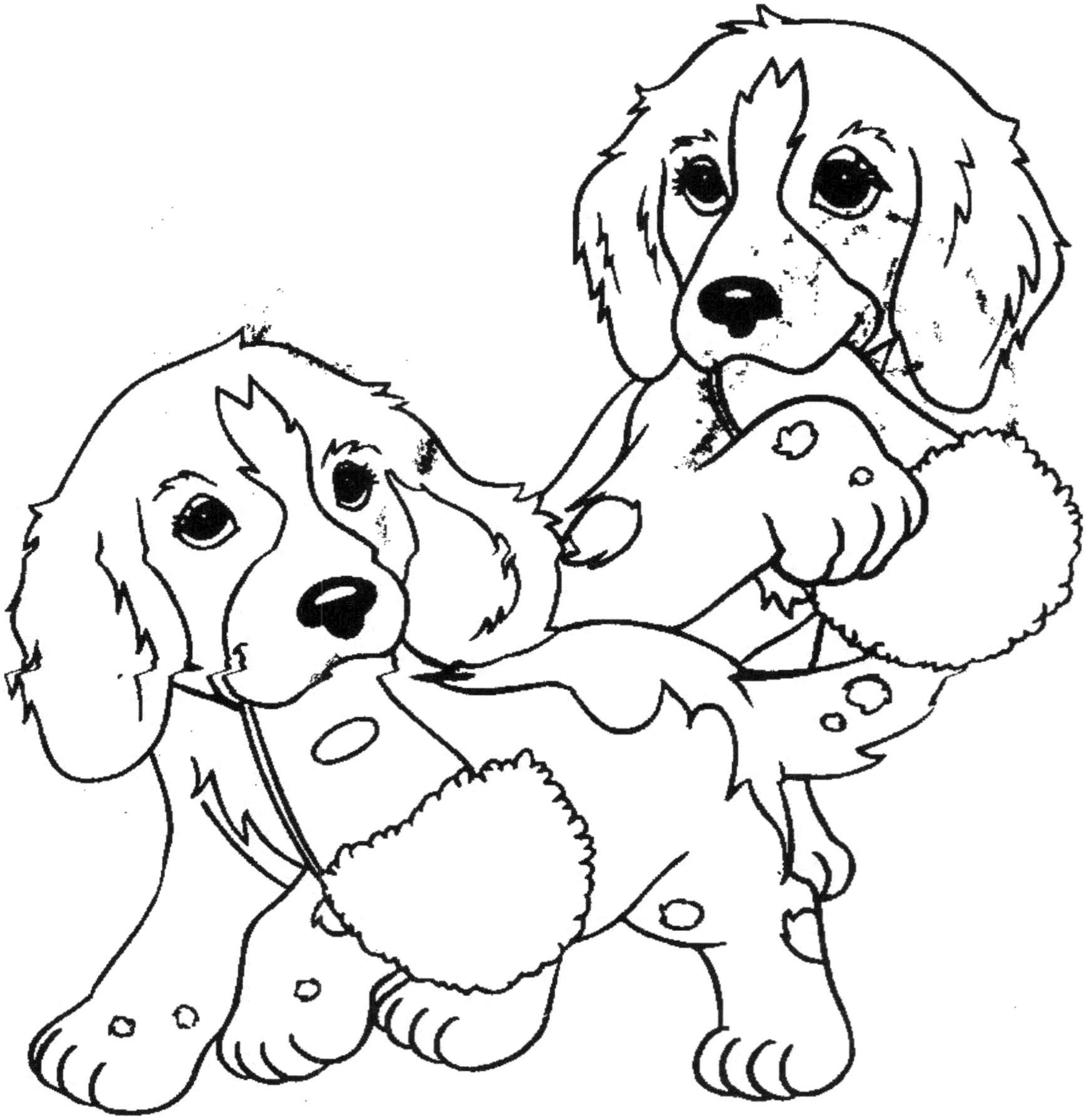

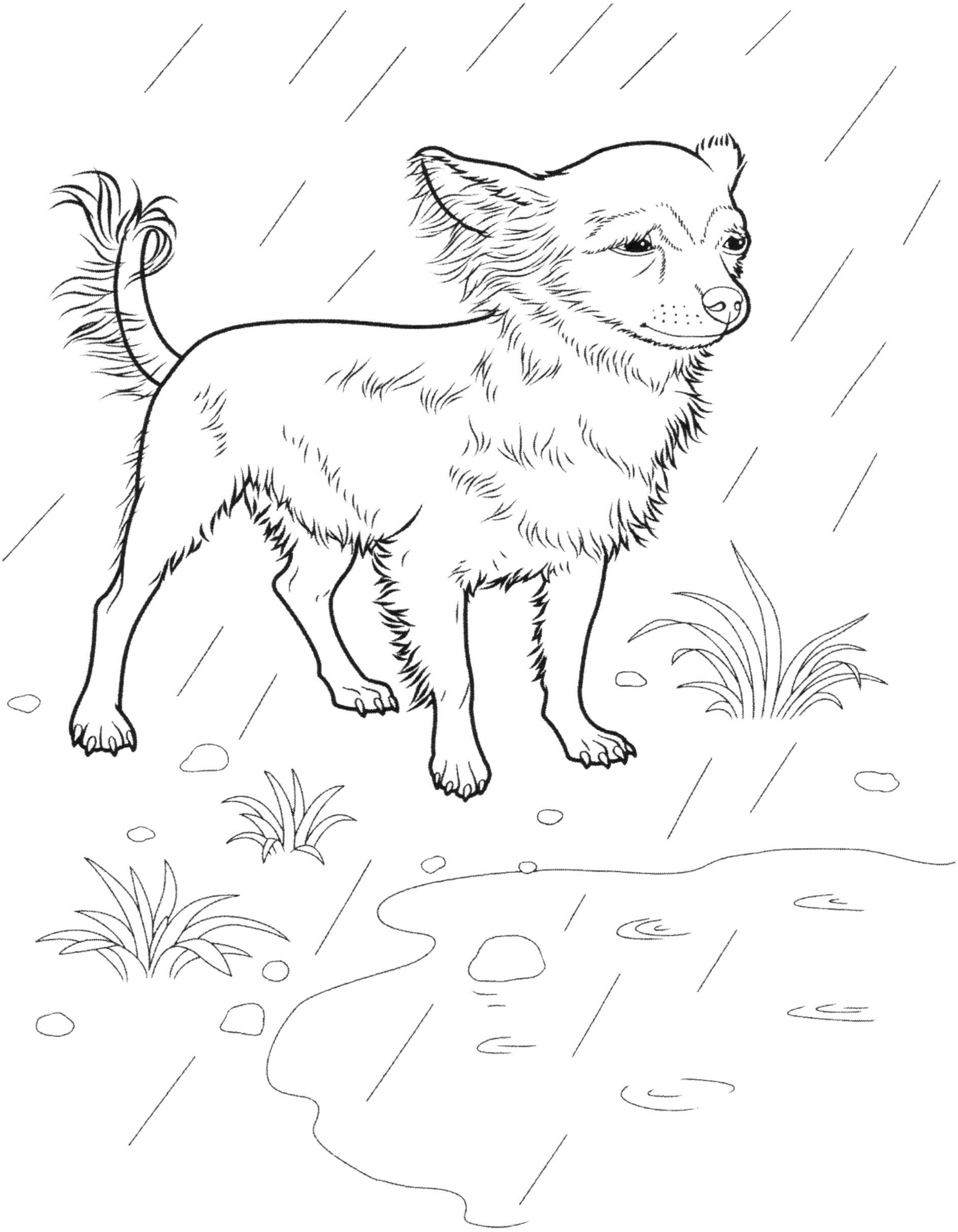

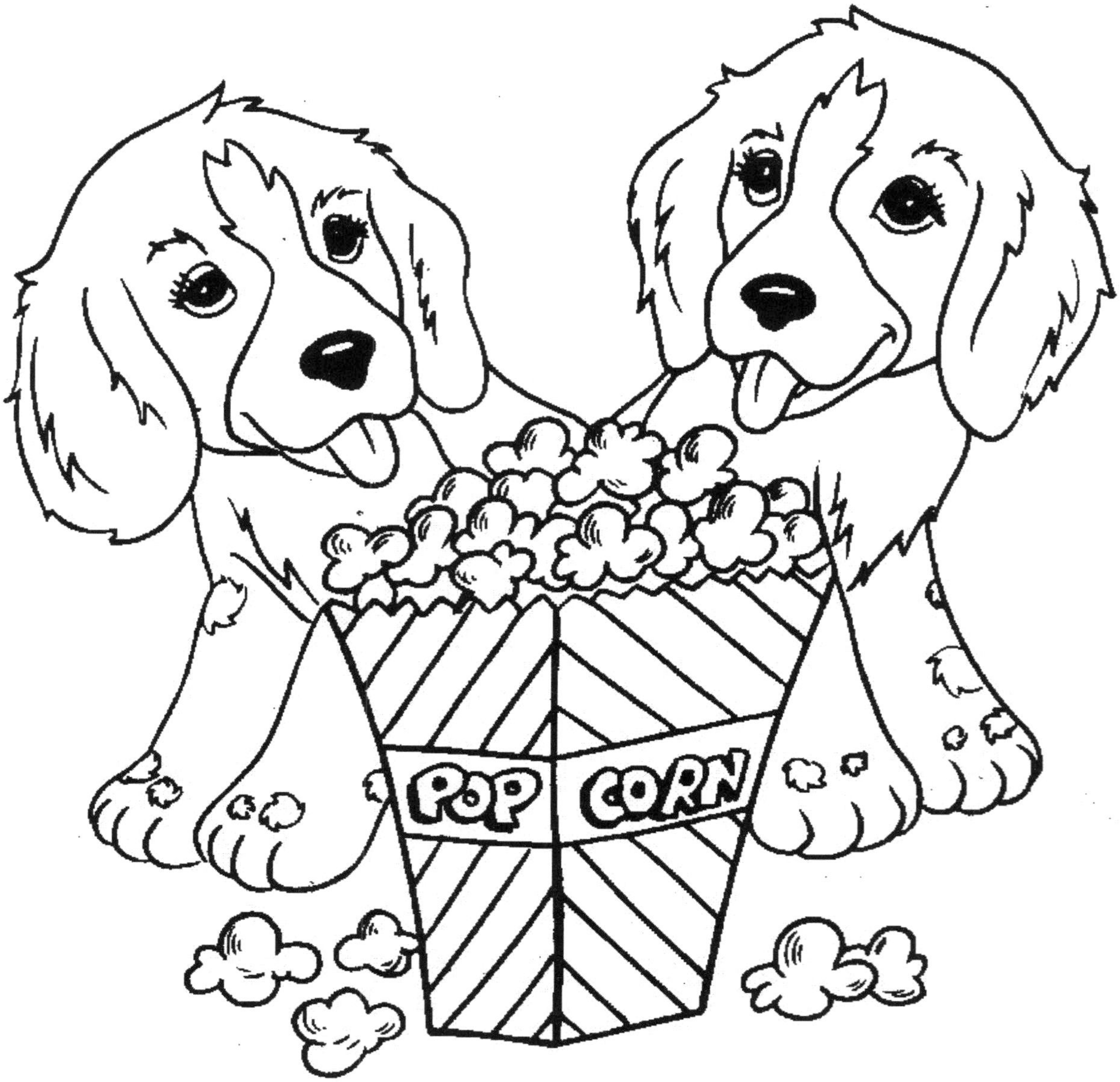
POP CORN

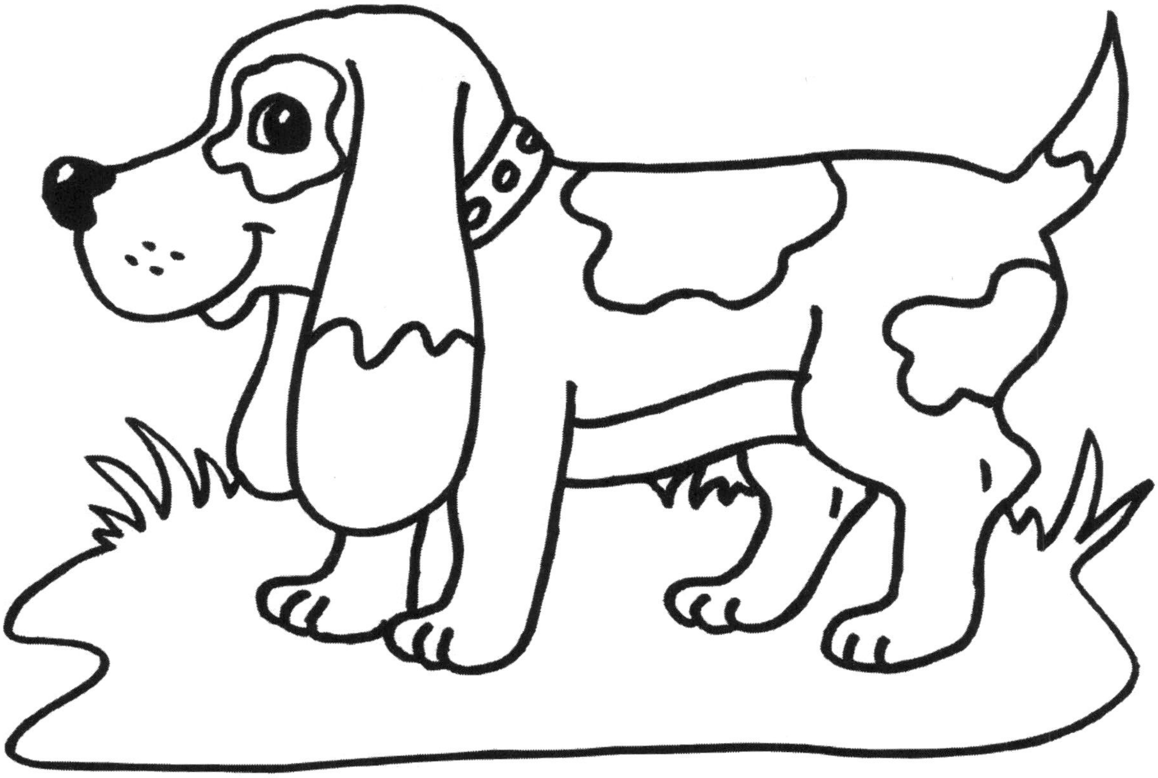

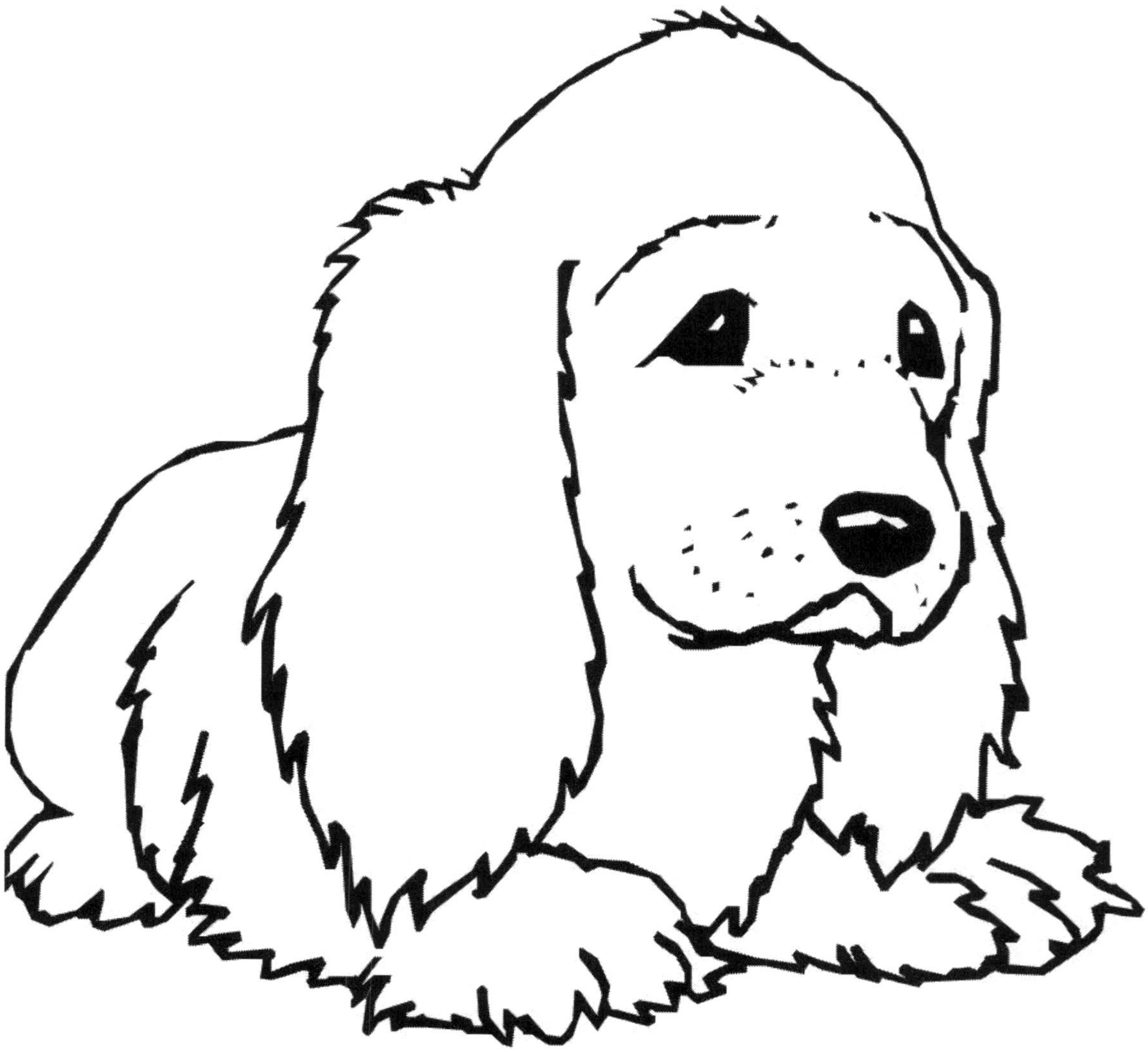

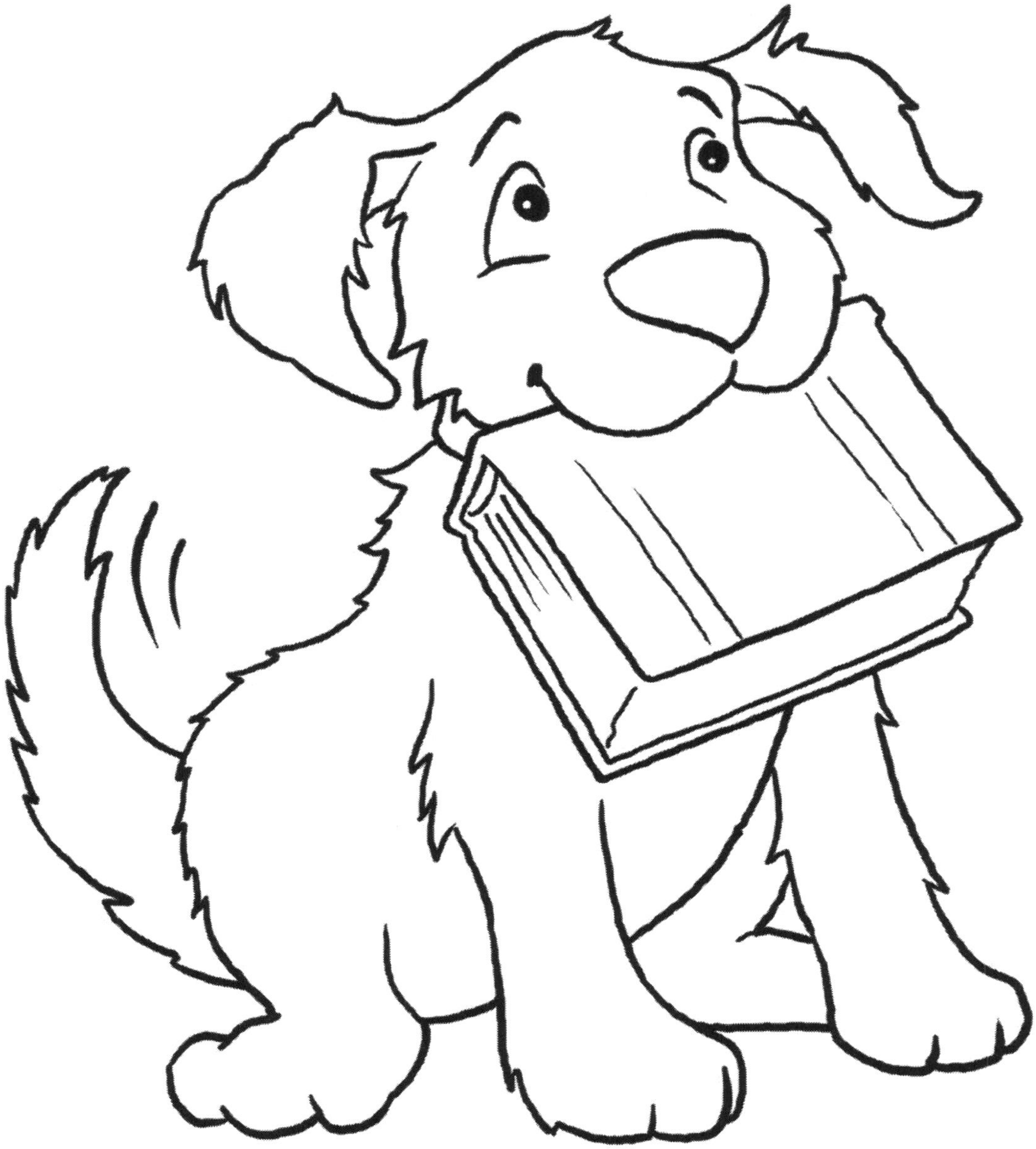

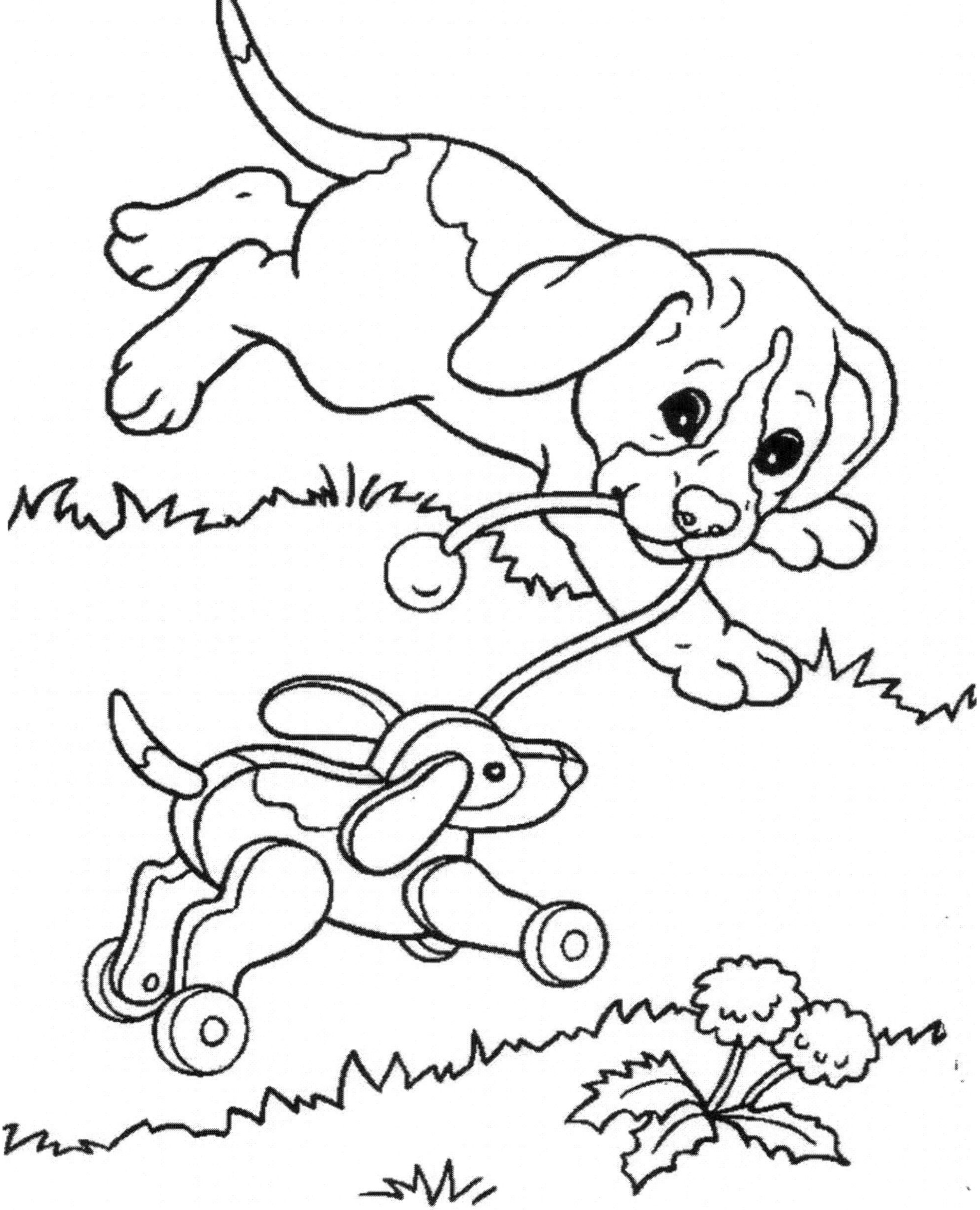

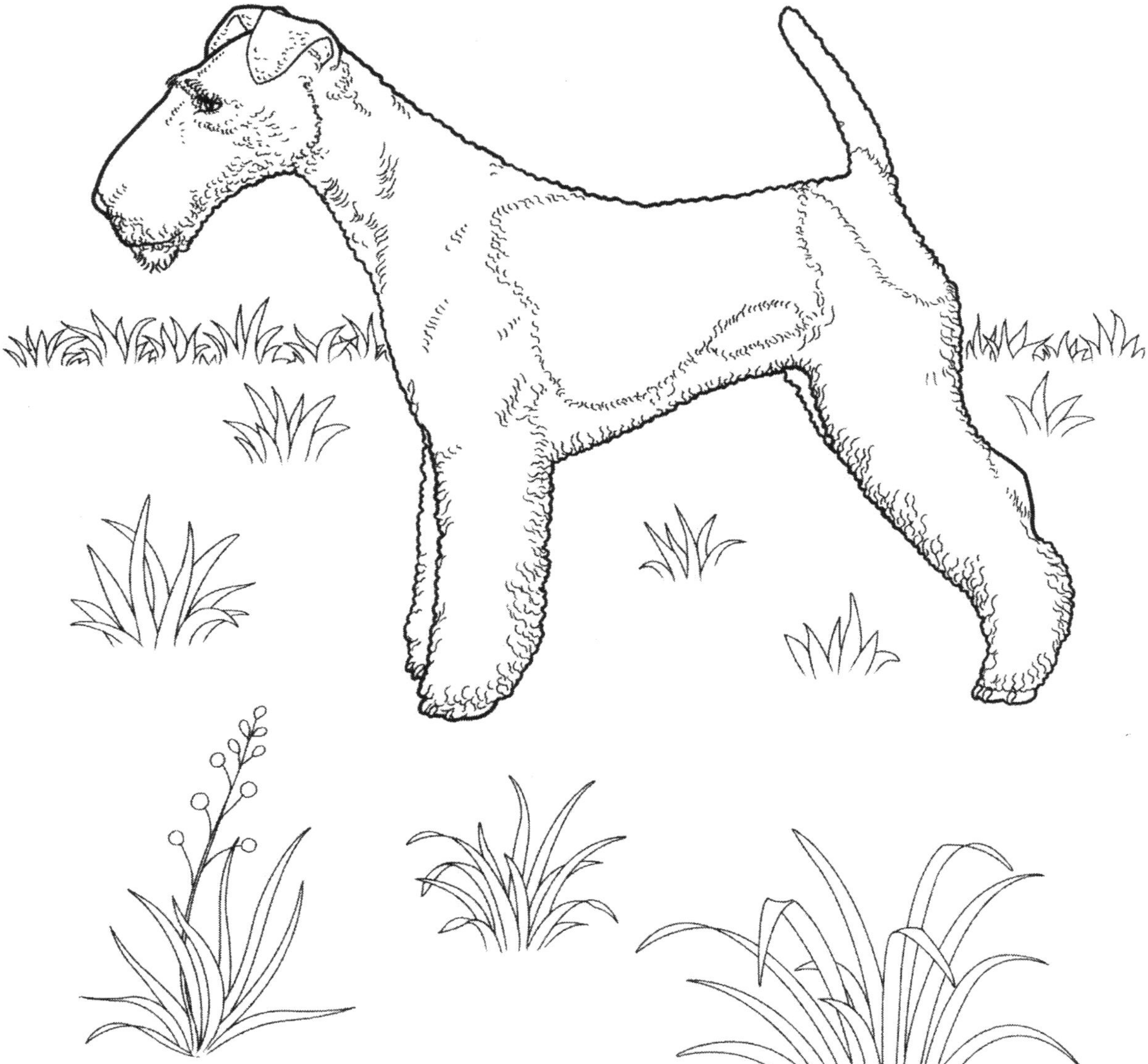

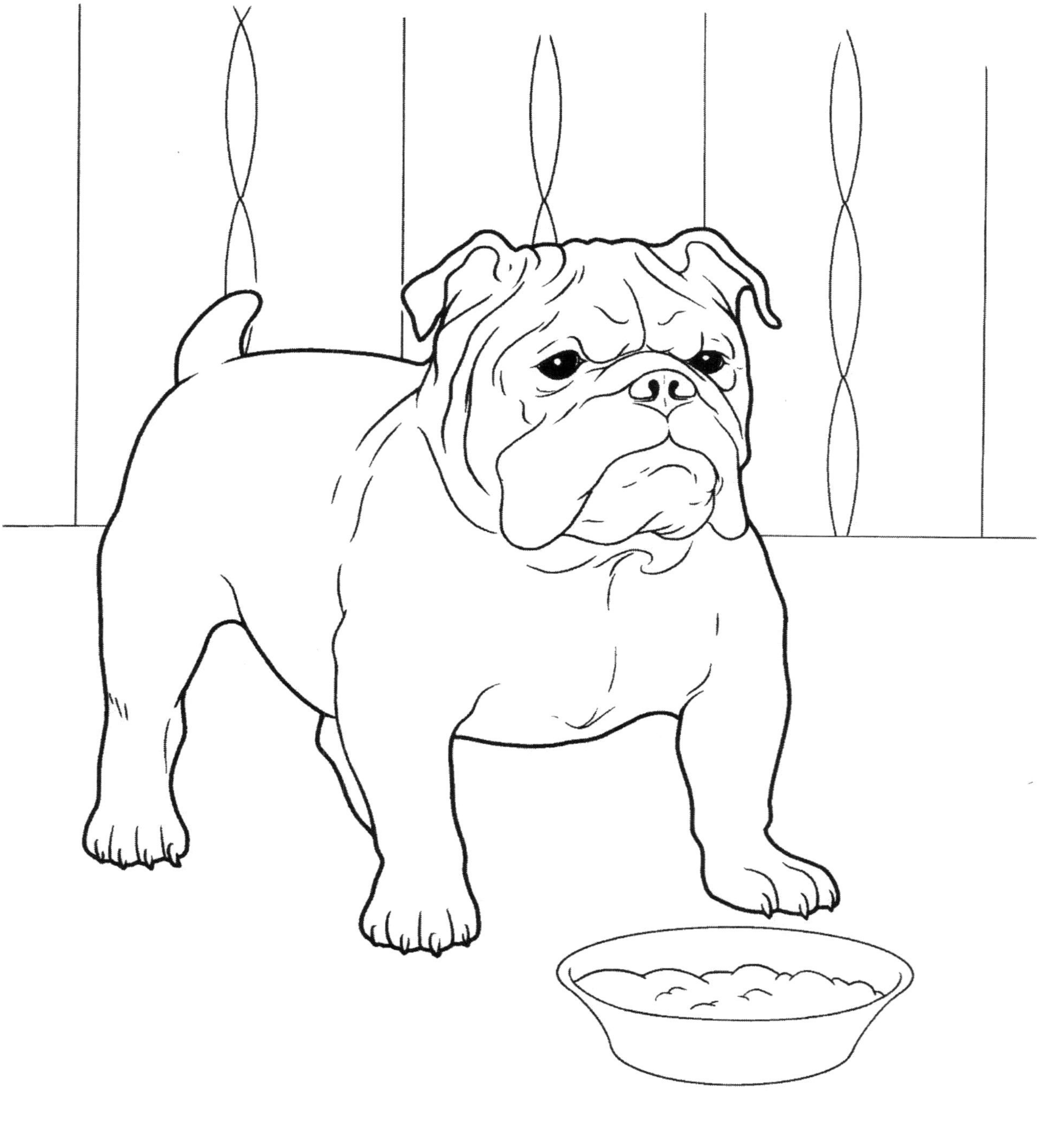

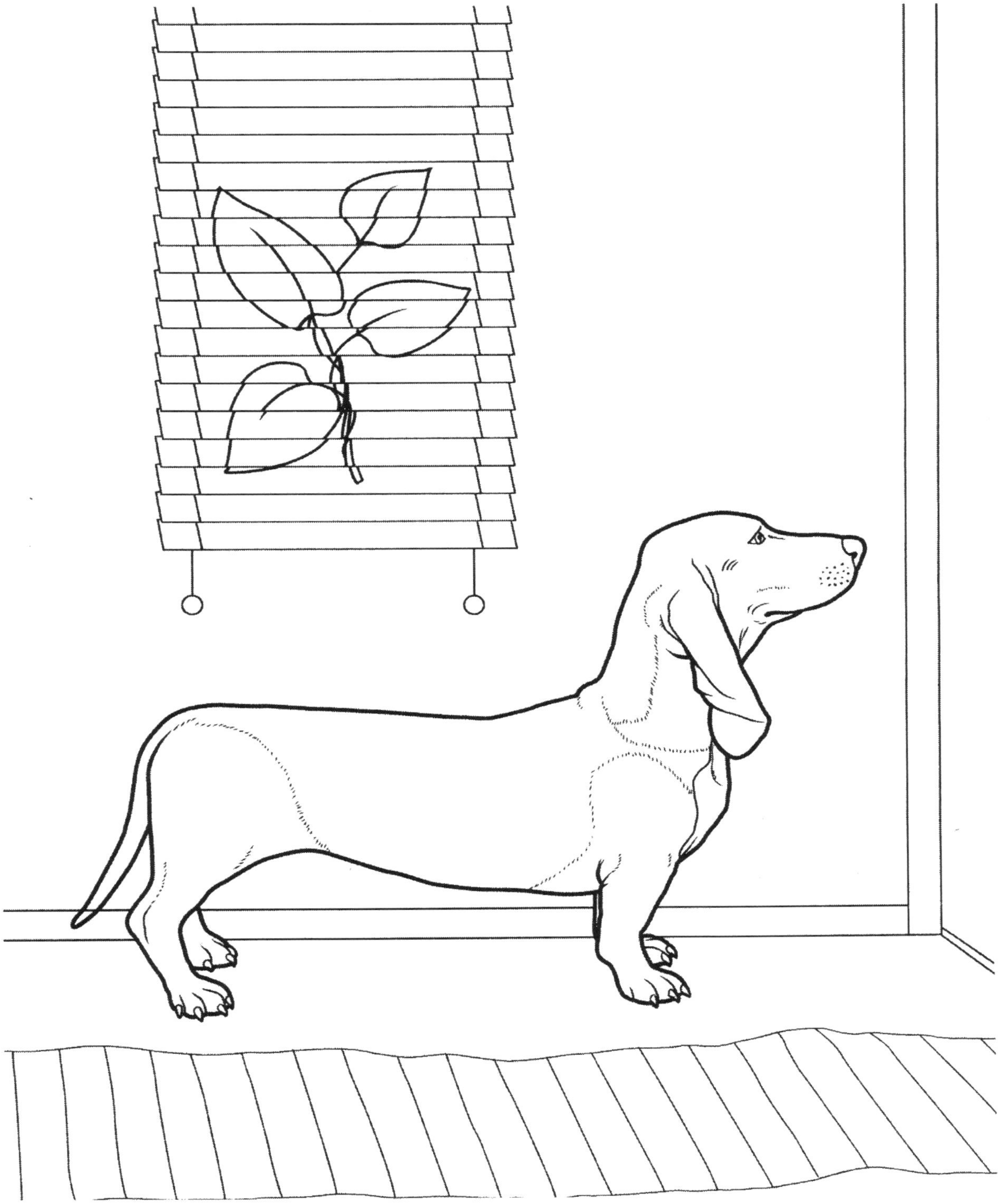

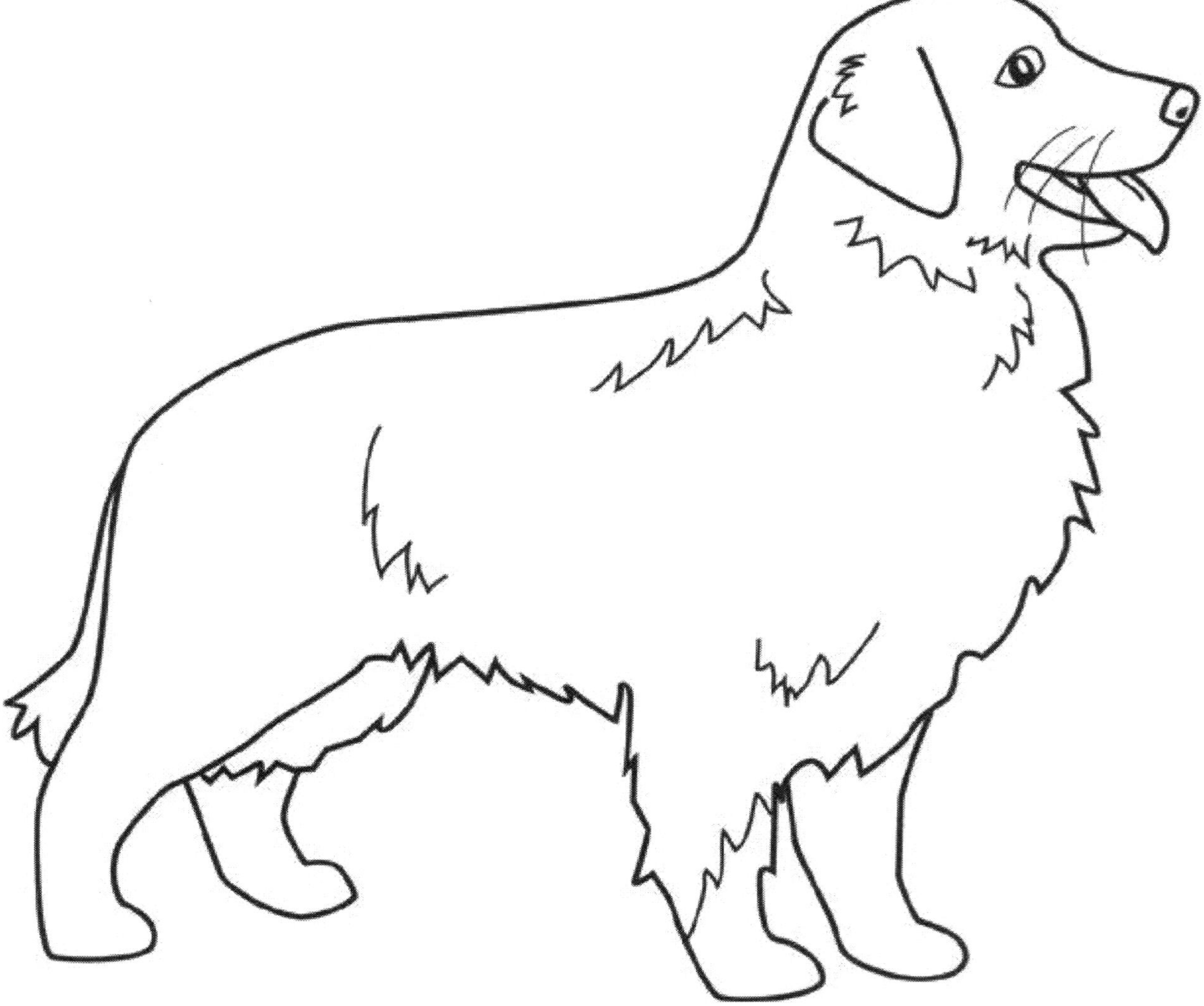

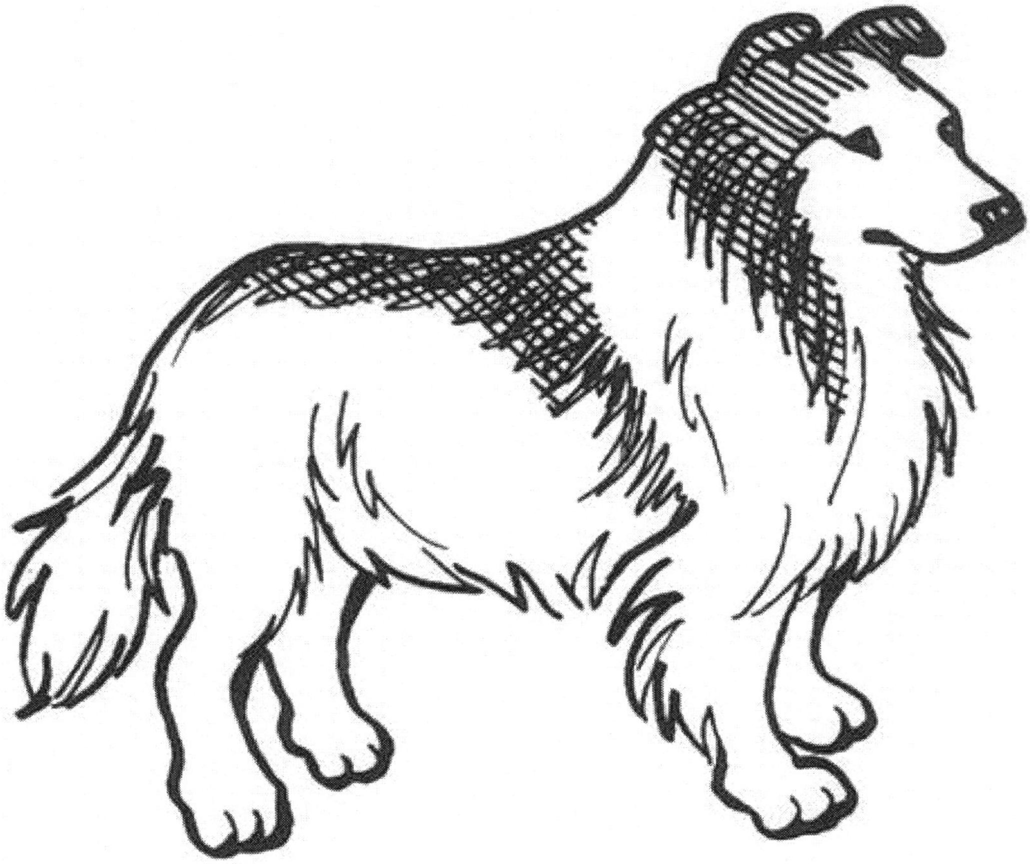

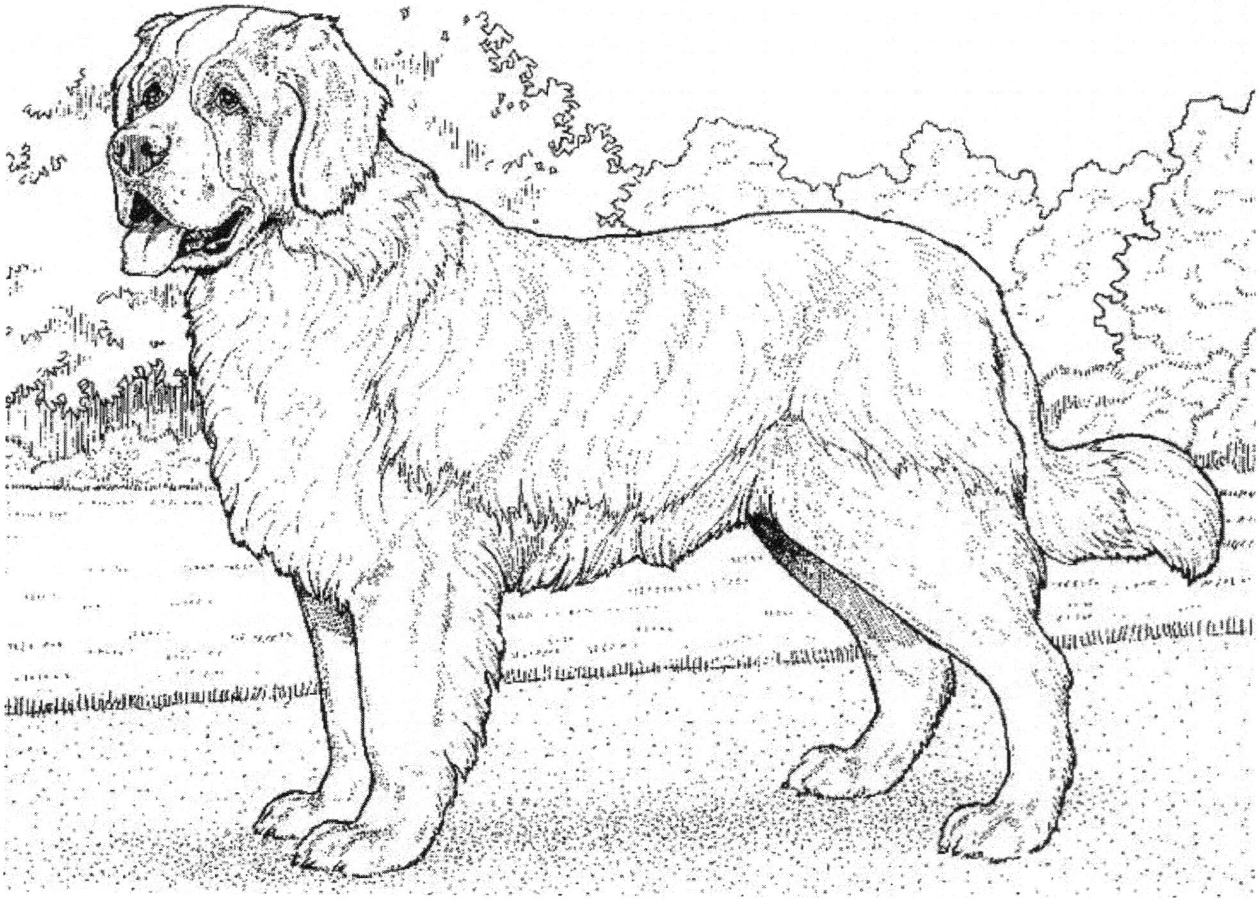

45502168R00027

Made in the USA
Charleston, SC
22 August 2015